Robert Gullifer read English at Cambridge and did his postgraduate education training at Oxford. He is currently director of the New College School Foundation. He has taught in both state and private sectors and has over twenty years' experience of senior leadership in secondary and primary schools. He now serves on the governing boards of several schools in the UK and is a Fellow of the Royal Society of Arts.

To Louise, Emma and Hetty, who, with tireless patience, support, and good humour, have lived with what it is to lead a school.

Robert Gullifer

How to Lead a School

Austin Macauley Publishers
LONDON · CAMBRIDGE · NEW YORK · SHARJAH

Copyright © Robert Gullifer 2022

The right of Robert Gullifer to be identified as author of this work has been asserted by the author in accordance with sections 77 and 78 of the Copyright, Designs and Patents Act 1988.

All rights reserved. No part of this publication may be reproduced, stored in a retrieval system, or transmitted in any form or by any means, electronic, mechanical, photocopying, recording, or otherwise, without the prior permission of the publishers.

Any person who commits any unauthorised act in relation to this publication may be liable to criminal prosecution and civil claims for damages.

Names, characters, businesses, places, events, locales, and incidents are either the products of the author's imagination or used in a fictitious manner. Any resemblance to actual persons, living or dead, or actual events is purely coincidental.

A CIP catalogue record for this title is available from the British Library.

ISBN 9781528951784 (Paperback)
ISBN 9781528960410 (ePub e-book)

www.austinmacauley.com

First Published 2022
Austin Macauley Publishers Ltd®
1 Canada Square
Canary Wharf
London
E14 5AA

I would not even have thought about writing this book had I not benefitted over many decades from the good counsel and unstinting encouragement of all the heads, chairs, school boards, teaching and support colleagues with whom I have worked. As a junior member of staff, then in senior leadership and headship, and latterly as a governor, I have been fortunate to learn from leaders of outstanding humanity and integrity who have greatly influenced the spirit of this book.

I should like to pay particular tribute to the trustees and governors with whom I have worked. Both individually and collectively, they have supported my educational priorities and have been a good part of enabling the fulfilment of leading a school.

Many fellow educationalists and senior leaders have kindly taken an interest in this project, but I would especially like to thank four distinguished colleagues and friends: Matt Jenkinson, Roger and Cheryl Trafford, and Ian Walker who have taken the trouble to read the book and make helpful suggestions and comments. All opinions and views, faults and shortcomings, of course, remain my own.

Table of Contents

Introduction	11
Chapter 1: Getting Started	13
Chapter 2: Students	26
Chapter 3: Teachers	40
Chapter 4: Senior Leadership Team	54
Chapter 5: The School Board	63
Chapter 6: Parents and Carers	73
Chapter 7: Support Staff	85
Chapter 8: The Wider Community	94
Chapter 9: Strategic Planning	103
Chapter 10: Looking After Yourself	113
Conclusion	120

Introduction

This is not another manual on leadership theory, but is written from experience as an informal, readable guide to the areas of school life and different constituencies a new school leader is likely to encounter. Addressed directly to the reader, it aims to give practical advice about the pleasures and pitfalls that are typically part of the job.

Leading a school is arguably one of those jobs which can only really be understood by doing it and living it. So this book gives an insider view. It endorses good practice and is designed to encourage and forearm you as you get started. It asks questions which are designed to provoke your thinking about key issues and helps you to survey the landscape ahead. It includes focused imaginary case studies of some of the sorts of situations you might encounter. There is also a look at the sort of characters who might be encountered on the way, some reminders of what is important, what is less so, and why the job is worth doing.

When starting to take charge of a school can at times seem overwhelming, chapter by chapter this book takes you calmly through the first few crucial things you ought to do and passes on some tricks of the trade. It aims to be a voice of professional solidarity so as both to affirm your best instincts and also give you a sense of perspective when the going gets tough. It is a huge responsibility and yet a hugely rewarding job to run a school: this book will help you make the most of it.

Chapter 1
Getting Started

*What's your vision? Getting to know the territory. Ten things to do before you start; and ten things **not** to do before you start. Setting out your stall.*

You've honed your CV or resumé. You've written a stonkingly good letter of application, subtly drawing attention to how your skills just fit the job. You've been grilled by school board trustees or governors in a couple of rounds of interviews, which have included being on your best behaviour to meet staff and possibly parents, and maybe even endured trial by canapé. And, congratulations, you've got the job. So now the real work begins. What's your vision for the school and how are you going to take it forward over the next decade or so?

You'll have thought about this, of course, in preparation for your interview. But you can't really have an authentic vision until you begin to experience the place on a daily basis and understand its nuances and foibles. But what you must first acknowledge, as part of your distinctive vision, is your own educational and professional hinterland.

It's a truism that everyone thinks they know about education just because they've been to school, but it's likely that you will have reflected particularly intently upon your own school days. What was good and what was bad about them will influence how you run things. Similarly, your experience in the schools you've worked in so far will guide you: your own experience in the classroom, your observations of senior leaders as a junior member of staff, and then as part of the leadership team itself. What would you imitate and what would you change? What appears easy, but could prove tricky? And then, to borrow from Shakespeare, 'to thine own self be true'. In an age when the moral compass of some leaders seems not to matter, the moral compass of a school leader is crucial. You'll be called upon to make judgments about all sorts of things and those judgements will be scrutinised by all those around you. Some of your judgements will be better than others, but so long as you make decisions with integrity (i.e. without bias and with objective moral principles), with single-minded concern to do what is right for the pupils and consistent with the values for which you are known and for which you have been appointed, you will sleep easier at night.

So, how do you get to know the new terrain? First of all, in a good handover, you will have had some useful conversations with your predecessor. This ought to include the practical stuff about school routines, the more subjective stuff about 'difficult' personalities and some honesty about problems unresolved. Not that you'll want to follow every bit of their advice – you need to make your own decisions about things for which you are now responsible – but it will give you some useful signposts. Similarly, conversations with each responses, rather than aimless whingeing. Needless to say, whatever approach you take, strict anonymity must be preserved.

It seems obvious to say that the best way to get to know your new school is to be out and about in it, but too often you can be deluged by emails and meetings and policy documents all aimed at grabbing the new leader's attention. So, make sure you put specific time in the diary to walk around the school at different times of the day. What's it like during lesson times, at change of lessons, at lunchtime, at the beginning and end of the day? Explain to teaching staff that you will want to drop into lessons not only with prospective parents, but because you are genuinely interested in the subject/the pedagogy aside from any formal observations: then going into lessons becomes not a big deal.

Getting to know existing parents personally is harder, but well worth the effort of finding out their expectations in the early days of your leadership. Try to bump into them for a few words on the sports field or at school shows or concerts rather than waiting for the first parents' evening. Parents dropping off and picking up younger pupils often value a quick chat in the school yard or playground.

As you walk around, don't forget to keep your eyes open for the state of the school's resources, large and small. Are the classroom arrangements fit for purpose? How welcoming is the entrance to the school? Are there corners of the school where bullying could go undetected? And what is the state of the toilets and washrooms…? The staff coffee facilities at break times…? But there's an important caveat here. It's beguilingly easier to deal with inanimate resources rather than human beings in all their loveable unpredictability. And of the senior leadership team and as many of the trustees as possible will give a good flavour of how things are.

And then there's nothing like a bit of homework. As principal or head, you rightly have privileged access to all documentation relating to pupils and staff and, of course, the accounts! It's worth having a good read through the files to see what issues are lurking or might inform your future planning. That's worth doing before you meet all the staff. In a large school, it's probably best if you arrange to attend a department or faculty meeting or a meeting of support staff with the specific agenda of listening to their aspirations for development, or simply their gripes about their current lot! In a small school, however, this could be done by individual meetings. But do remember first, how much teachers resent purposeless meetings and second, how some staff intrinsically worry about being asked to meet the boss: so make sure you (and your PA) are benignly clear on precise timings and the straightforward fact-finding/listening agenda. And why not have a party or two? Everyone likes parties and it can be a great way to break the ice with parents and staff and signal the start of a new era.

Many schools these days routinely undertake surveys of parents and carers, and often pupils and staff too. Some schools appoint external consultants to do this with often quite detailed questions about wide-ranging aspects of a school's operation. Some schools carry out internal surveys modelled on the questionnaires used by an inspectorate or quality review bodies; others simply ask respondents to give, say, five aspects of school life they value and five aspects they would like to see developed further. The latter approach is certainly very simple to administer and encourages constructive whilst buildings and material resources make a difference, your primary focus should always be on people. They are your most valuable resource and they should always be uppermost in your vision.

One area you'll probably have forgotten to survey initially is the overall educational landscape of your locality. What are the neighbouring schools like? How do they impinge on your operation? Could you find some soul mates in your fellow heads or principals through a local or professional association network? Why not consider asking if you could visit their school at an early opportunity?

There's a lot to take in when you first arrive, so jot down your first impressions on all of this before you forget. (It's useful to keep a note on your phone if you're on the move round the school campus). Then take time over the first few months to think how your findings relate to your long-term vision.

Nonetheless, as a new leader, you'll be in a rush to 'get things done', to show you're in charge, and to establish your credentials as someone who will make a difference. All that is laudable and understandable, but you'll need to be careful about making rash decisions at an early stage before you've really got under the skin of the place. Conventional leadership advice has tended to be along the lines of wait and see what happens for a year and then introduce your vision. But in the life of a pupil, a year is crucial and you may well be unequivocally convinced that some tweaks will be worth doing straightaway. So, don't be afraid: it's all a matter of balance.

Here are ten suggestions of the sort of things you might well do before or just as you start:

- Meet with the chair of the school board informally and find out what governors/trustees see as current priorities. You will have picked up some of these at interview, but individual discussion may be more revealing and builds up an important relationship of trust between you and the chair.
- Meet the bursar or finance officer and get a thorough understanding of how the school's finances work. It's important to establish a very good working relationship from the start.
- Go through every page on the school's website to make sure everything is up-to-date and reflects the image of the school you want to project.
- Check that all policy documents, especially safeguarding, are in order and that all staff training is up-to-date. You don't want to be blind-sided by any inspection in your first term and you might see a need to ensure updated training on your first INSET day.
- Discuss with your PA how you would best like to work with them. What routines are there already? Will these work for you? Who handles emails? Your diary? Decide what regular meetings you want with key staff. Are there too many meetings? Too few?
- Make sure you understand as far as possible the role that every member of staff carries out and try to meet with most of them just before or as you start. You want to be sure to delegate and mete out appropriate

praise to the correct people right from the start. First impressions of a new leader count.

- The school board will already have sent parents formal notification of your appointment, but a friendly letter from you at the beginning of term, telling them a little bit more about your background and interests, thanking them for their support for the school and perhaps offering an early opportunity to meet at a social gathering. This will go a long way to satisfy parents' natural curiosity about you.
- You are very much going to be public property in the community. So why not make a virtue of it and get a few column inches in the local newspaper? All good for the profile of the school and for pupil recruitment.
- Check that you understand the daily routines and timetable and check for any inconsistencies or inefficiencies in timings or staffing which might be addressed sooner rather than later for the benefit of pupils' learning and welfare.
- Lastly, if there's something which really doesn't fit with the way you want to do things or the values you want to promote, be bold enough to make an immediate, manageable change provided you explain the demonstrable benefits of what you are doing to all constituencies. There's usually a brief 'honeymoon period' for a new head, so make the most of it!

But, as first steps, I suggest you **do not**:

- Fire your PA because they keep referring to how things were done in the past. For parents and

colleagues, your PA often represents a reassuring continuity at the heart of the school at a time of change. Moreover, some historic knowledge, however irrelevant it may seem at times, can prove vital in managing a good number of issues.
- Introduce a new management structure. You'll have no senior allies if you do.
- Have an expensive refit of your office. Be demonstrably cost effective or make it clear to colleagues/parents that you've paid for some improvements yourself.
- Tinker with the timings of the start and end of the school day. Monolithic family arrangements often depend on them.
- Change the curriculum provision or balance between subjects. There are usually major vested interests here which need careful unravelling.
- Change the uniform, however repelled you are by the colour of the sports kit. Parents like to make uniform last and resent having it changed on a whim.
- Reform the rewards and sanctions policy. Since you must rely on colleagues to apply the policy fairly, you need to get their buy-in first.
- Attempt anything contentious to do with parking for staff or parents before you understand the no-doubt irrational custom and practice which have built up over time.
- Announce plans for a new performance management system. Unless there are widespread problems of underperformance, this smacks of management

control and not professional trust. The latter is what really good teachers prize, so don't alienate the good ones at the start.
- Insist on elaborate control of things like photocopying. Whilst there may be pressure from the finance department to rationalise this cost centre, micro-managing teaching resources undermines professional judgment. And no system will ever take into account the genuinely differing needs of different departments. Much better to appeal to teachers' professionalism and give them ownership of the collective responsibility for prudent budgeting.

So, all eyes are on you. There's an expectation in the air. What does the new appointee think about X or Y? What's the future going to be like under this new leadership? Time to set out your stall. You will obviously do this formally over the next few months in a well-considered and widely-consulted development plan, but there's also a need for a drip-drip feed of ideas in more subtle ways. So use every communication trick in the book to get across the essentials of what you stand for, what you believe in, and what floats your educational boat. Regular newsletters don't have to be a dull account of what's happened this week and what's going to happen next week. Even if that's the outline structure, there's still plenty of scope to comment on pupils' responses to what is going on in a way which will identify your educational priorities. Similarly, the pithy tweet or re-tweet will reveal many of your interests to the wider world. You can often get the message across, too, by giving your take on local and/or national educational initiatives, but be careful not to be too controversial until you really know your audience. Your first INSET day will also be a chance to trail some of your ideas and to judge initial reactions from staff. It's also a chance to find out what their priorities are and get a feeling for how you will bring together your (probably longer-term) vision and their (probably shorter-term) wish-list.

You're enthused and ready to go. You've got an exciting plan. Now to bring it to life with all the human and material resources with whom/which you've been entrusted. Your job is to keep all the plates spinning, to keep the place purring along in Rolls-Royce style. You'll spend a lot of time listening as well as doing. There'll be lots of frustrating bumps in the road, as well as the hugely rewarding satisfaction of seeing the way smoothed for the intellectual and emotional development of the young lives that are the reason for doing all this in the first place. If you do everything with their wellbeing in mind, you won't go too far wrong. That's why they come top of my list of the various school constituencies who are the subjects of the subsequent chapters of this book.

******

Lettie Prism has just been appointed head teacher of Cardew School, a one-form-entry rural primary school. In conversation with the chair of her school board, she has been given a clear view that the board has been concerned about school/parent communication, with one parent, who is also a trustee, asserting that she generally felt very unwelcome in the school. A number of parents have said that the head only seems to have limited time to see them and that emails get filtered by the school office.

Lettie has decided to take the following actions:

- *Ask the chair of the parents' association if parents would be willing to organise a 'Meet the New Head' drinks party, and encourage attendance from as many parents as possible.*
- *Start a weekly newsletter, including photos and video clips of school life.*
- *Increase the school's presence on social media.*
- *Be on duty at the school gate (or ensure her deputy is, if she is away) at drop-off and pick-up time.*
- *Hold a training session for office staff on positive approaches with parents on the phone, by email, in person.*
- *Ask her PA to forward all non-routine emails from parents and put a daily half-hour slot in the diary to go through how responses will be dealt with.*
- *Reserve a dedicated after-school diary slot for potential parent meetings on two/three days a week.*
- *Delegate some of her regular meetings with members of staff to her deputy.*
- *Review the policy for parents visiting the school to encourage support for assemblies, individual music lessons, learning support etc.*
- *Set up a termly 'Show and Tell' session for each class at pick-up time.*

- *Invite members of the school board to spend a morning/afternoon in school observing lessons.*

As she implements these ideas, she comes up against the following difficulties:

- *The parents' association has been rather moribund in recent years because of a lack of interest from the head and nobody seems willing to organise any social events.*
- *IT expertise and resources for an elaborate newsletter or social media presence are limited in the school office.*
- *Her PA has been used to a default position that the head's diary needs to be protected and asserts that parents are inherently difficult and that training for a more positive approach will make no difference.*
- *Staff are anxious about members of the school board coming in to observe lessons.*

With some further creative thinking, Lettie decides:

- *To appeal for a parent representative from each class to meet with her to plan a re-invigoration of the parents' association with a remit to be a source of advice on school issues as well as organising social occasions. But she puts a meet-the-head party firmly on the agenda too.*
- *To ask one of the class teachers, who seems to use social media very fluently, to take on the responsibility of promoting the school on social*

media and acting as 'school photographer'. A small money and/or time allowance will need to be arranged.

- *That, notwithstanding her PA's mindset, he is an efficient administrator and well-liked by teaching and support staff, so it would not be prudent to replace him for the time being. But Lettie insists that all parents be given an appointment as soon as there is space in her diary and makes it her intention to check up on this in conversation with parents at the school gate.*
- *That during the first few school board visits, Lettie will lead by example and that visitors will sit in and observe her lessons, but will be given a brief tour of the school to drop in to other lessons.*

Chapter 2
Students

Safeguarding and wellbeing. Ethos of the school in practice. The students' experience: pastoral care; the school environment; student feedback. Making sure the students know you. Your philosophy of teaching and learning. The curriculum. 'Wrap-around' care. Learning support. Disciplinary matters. Positive celebration.

You will know that the most important responsibility you have as head is the safeguarding of the young people in your care. Others will have specific and legal roles in this, such as your school's safeguarding lead and the local safeguarding officers, but you are the person whose judgements and decisions will have significant influence on how effectively they can carry out their roles. And the signals you give out about the importance of safeguarding (in all its manifestations) for everyone in the organisation are crucial. A scary responsibility? But none more vital as a bedrock for children's happy growth and development. You will have done the courses, including safer recruitment of staff, and checked that the procedures so neatly set down in the school's safeguarding policy are understood by all and are fit for purpose. But how can you ascertain that there really is a school culture in which students are comfortable to share concerns? Getting feedback via wellbeing lessons is a good starting point, as is a student questionnaire of the sort often used by inspectors. Will staff really know what to do on the spur of a moment? A quick digest on a pocket-sized card is a helpful prompt which some schools provide for staff to carry around for just such unforeseen moments when a child discloses. Above all, then, as with so many aspects of school life, you have to be certain that policy translates into practice. That will mean you and your pastoral leaders repeating the message clearly and often, and listening for feedback. Then what might seem a scary responsibility becomes less scary because you'll know you've done as much as you can to ensure that safeguarding is taken seriously, and robustly supported.

You may have a clear idea of the ethos (that 'catch-all' word encapsulating values and USP) of the school, but unless that is taken to heart and demonstrated by the students in all they do, it will remain an empty aspiration and not have the desired educational effect. The reality in any school is that, whilst you can set the tone, it's the students who will show it (or not) in action. So how do you start to make sure that the ethos of the place is worked out in practice? As any good teacher knows, an 'I say, you do' approach produces an immediate contrary response in even very young children. You have to start by modelling the values yourself. If, for example, you want students to be more considerate in the corridors, why don't you hold doors open for them? They might be a bit surprised at first, shamed even, but there's an important subliminal message here: nobody is too important or too busy to be courteous and kind to others. If you want them to be punctual in completing homework, make sure in turn you are rigorously punctual in marking and returning work. If you want them to wear their uniform smartly, dress smartly yourself. It's obvious really: children are quick to scent out double standards and so you'll also need to make sure all adults in the community are as consistently 'on-message' as possible.

And don't forget that the physical environment of a school has a profound effect on pupils and how they go about their work and play in school. If you want a quiet school, how about switching off the school bells and making students and teachers responsible for the prompt start and end of lessons? The Pavlovian reaction of students shuffling their belongings and the noise of the school bell are thus avoided. How are the classrooms or learning spaces arranged? Could some discussions with the teachers who use them bring about changes in layout, which would benefit the students? Equally, try to think about the shape and size of the school yard, the nature of the equipment in it. Does it suit all interests, all ages? Is there space for sitting and talking, as well as running around. Are there any spaces hidden from view where bullying might take place? Is there a library or reading area inside where students can go at break time? Is it a welcoming or forbidding place? And what about lunch? A rushed, loud and cramped experience, or time for conversation and healthy digestion? With your new eyes on it all, small, cost-effective improvements can quickly make a difference.

One of the quickest ways to find out whether or not the pupils' experiences reflect the core values of the school is to shadow perhaps two or three students from different age groups for half a day or so. First, it's a timely reminder of how, in most years in school, they are rapidly switching from one subject to another and often travelling between classrooms, too, with multiple belongings. This has its own challenges for many. Second, you get to see a variety of lessons and teachers and learning environments in action. Third, once chosen students have been reassured you're not checking up on them personally, you have a chance to talk to them informally about their aspirations and outlook and send the all-important message that you care about the children in the school, just as much as the adults.

Most schools also have more formal structures in place to garner student views. A school council is often a valuable sounding board and students are eager to make suggestions about all sorts of things they really care about. Some students might prefer to do this more anonymously through a suggestions box. Some suggestions can be hopelessly impractical or of partisan interest, but much can be of real assistance in your development planning. It's important that you go along to council meetings from time to time, perhaps even chair meetings, to acknowledge suggestions and give considered responses to all, even if you have gently to point out the impossibility of some of the wackier ideas. And the starting point for all meetings should be: 'How can we make our school better?'

Probably one of the greatest adjustments you'll have to make on taking charge of the school is simply not teaching as much as you did, even as part of a leadership team. Sadly, it takes you away from that very special and privileged interaction which first drew you into the teaching profession. On the other hand, you won't miss the marking…Opinions vary as to how much teaching a school principal or head should do, but the bottom line is that you need to be available to deal with the many matters that crop up in the in-tray, as and when they arrive. It simply doesn't serve the students well, and seriously annoys your colleagues, if your teaching has to be covered every time an irate parent arrives on your doorstep. But it is possible, and desirable, to build some teaching into your weekly schedule, if only to keep some of that vital contact with students and to prove to your colleagues that you can still set the pace. It's obviously not wise, unless absolutely necessary, to take an exam class or a core subject with a large number of lessons per week, but do try to take some time to get to know your new intake as they start at the school. Perhaps story time with a very junior class or a wellbeing/pastoral session with a more senior class.

Even in a very large school, you'll want to get to know as many of the students as quickly as possible. Whilst this obviously gets easier the longer you're in post, you'll need some strategies to get to grips with names and faces early on. Some new leaders invest a good deal of time studying photographs on databases; others visit a different class each week for the first term to join in registration – a handy way of hearing names matched to faces.

Students will also want to get to know you. The principal or head who doesn't have much contact with students instantly invites suspicion, even contempt. Busy though you may be in doing things for their benefit, if you're invisible except at assembly or just to the few classes you teach, you'll find it hard to win the loyalty of students which is vital to the day-to-day smooth running of the school. You'll probably front assembly on a regular basis, but why not actually take a few assemblies and use them as longer opportunities to share some of your interests? Rather touchingly, pupils love to know what makes their teachers tick and school leaders are no exception to this. Lunchtime is another opportunity for getting to know students. Whilst some schools have separate staff dining areas, there's no reason why you always have to eat with staff. Of course, students have an unerring habit of sliding quietly away as soon as the head or principal hoves into view, but older pupils may stay the course and, with luck and good judgment on your side, will report that the conversation with you was really quite interesting and in fact a chance to air a few opinions. More formally, many schools have established routines for school leaders to have lunch with selected pupils from different year groups across the academic year. Valuable in many ways, but inevitably a little more stilted and, unless you can cover a whole group in one year or have transparent selection criteria (e.g. form monitors, prefects etc.), students will wonder why some of them were included and some left out.

It may seem obvious to say that what will most affect the day-to-day life of a school's students is how they learn and what they learn in the classroom. Here, you ought to have a very clear philosophy of learning and teaching which may build on the school's existing approach or which may mean you have to begin to remodel it, according to local circumstances and demands. A fundamental judgement for any new school leader is to work out if the balance between teacher-led activities and independent learning is generally healthy across the school. Here, lesson observations early on will begin to inform your views. Are students easily able to access IT and library resources for independent research? Are homework tasks properly prepared for in class? Is there rather too much emphasis on worksheets and closed questions in classroom teaching? Even more fundamentally, is there an atmosphere of mutual respect in lessons which enables confident learning, or do pupils seem to be in fear of making mistakes or saying/doing the wrong thing? Now that the Covid pandemic has made online learning generally possible, rather than exceptional, there's no reason why you shouldn't insist on some lessons, or at least homework, being uploaded to a portal accessible to pupils and parents. And that's an easy way for you to gauge the quality of teaching.

As mentioned in the previous chapter, the balance of the curriculum is often a tricky area of school life with many embedded interests. Schools seem to have to add more and more into the curriculum as they respond to the latest best educational practice. But it's often difficult to take things away, which can lead to what might be regarded as the slightly tortuous solutions of a two-week timetable or other such compromises, which do not necessarily make the students' learning experience significantly better. Once you have got your feet under the table, it's a good idea to have a curriculum review. This needs to be a painstaking process, starting with an open statement of the parameters to all staff. Something along the lines of: 'In order to adopt best educational practice/to conform with latest legislation and serve our students best, we need to add this or that subject to the curriculum. We do not wish to extend the formal school day or shorten the break times, so how can we solve this problem collectively?' You'll be surprised how quickly some staff are willing to compromise because they see the bigger picture and they will be your allies in bringing on board those who are fearful of change. In the end, though, having genuinely listened, you and your senior curriculum leader(s) have to make the decision as to the best way in which the cookie should crumble.

As schools respond to the reality of dual-working parents, they are called upon more and more to provide 'wrap-around' care. Breakfast, Homework and Holiday Clubs abound. But on joining your new school, you'll need to make an assessment as to exactly how the nuts and bolts of this provision affect the wellbeing of students. First, are these clubs run by the teaching staff or by additional support staff? Does this make a difference to the adult/child dynamic? And how might this impact upon the school budget? Second, are these clubs to be educational or are they simply places in which children can be supervised before parents collect them? There's no right or wrong answer here, but you need to be clear with parents what the school is offering. And the provision will depend on the age group. Young children may need to have a quiet time after the stimulation of a school day and you may need to be firm with parents about not depending on extended child care if children are to be ready and alert for the following school day. Older children will benefit from more structured activity and, if possible, a chance to make their own choices about what interests they follow after the end of the formal school day. That makes for a much happier time for all. The sheer joy of students and teachers sharing interests in a more relaxed way is really good for the emotional temperature of the school and might just mean fewer disciplinary matters end up on your desk.

But, not infrequently, there will be the complexities and clashes and multiple demands of lots of different personalities co-existing in a relatively crowded environment. Children (and adults for that matter) all have their own hopes and fears, the baggage of existences and experiences beyond the school gate, which they bring with them into school. Schools have got much better over recent years in recognising that the first way to cope with problems which arise is focused academic and pastoral support. The days are fast disappearing now, thank goodness, when going to the learning support department was seen by students and parents as some sort of stigma. But if you're really putting students' wellbeing top of your list, you'll need to make sure that assessment for learning is truly working and that students are encouraged to know their strengths and weaknesses and where they can turn to for support. Some initial strategies might include having a drive on formative marking and getting students to respond to teachers' written comments. And how about widening the scope of learning support to include such sessions as how to revise for exams? Even more fundamentally, is the learning support department a bright and cheerful learning space at the centre of the school, or is it tucked away in a neglected corner? A bit of creative space-shuffling one school vacation could make all the difference to students' (and teachers') perceptions of learning needs. And, of course, fulfilled learners, rather than frustrated learners, make for a much more contented school environment.

You will know from your experience as a teacher just how interconnected a school's academic and pastoral provision are. Happy students make happy learners. You may have seen, perhaps as a form teacher, just how much more can be achieved in the classroom by sorting out pastoral problems, large and small. But part of a school leader's responsibility is to make sure that pastoral support is consistent across the school and that policies reflect clear stages of upward internal and external referral for more difficult and specialist problems. Clearly, this is first and foremost the remit of a pastoral deputy, but your creative and persuasive input may be needed if, for example, you need to convince the governors that more money needs to be spent in-house on services such as counselling or psychological assessments. Equally your fresh pair of eyes on policies might well contribute to greater clarity in an area of school life where procedures are often complex and delicate and can quickly accrete to the point of being not very user-friendly for busy teachers.

It may seem hopelessly liberal to say that most teachers believe in children's inherent capacity for good. And principals and heads certainly do. Indeed, you will often be the person who sees the bigger picture, slightly detached as you are from the immediate triggers of friction in the classroom or school yard. Schools and teachers have become much better at trying to understand and address what lies behind poor behaviour and you'll almost certainly have buy-in on this from most members of staff, without compromising the need to put down disciplinary markers as and when students need to be put back on track.

One of the more intractable pastoral/disciplinary things you'll almost certainly have to get to grips with in setting the tone is to try to get some measure of consistency in the way rewards and sanctions are handed out. A very prescribed list of scenarios will never cover *all* scenarios and so you have to trust the judgement of your colleagues. They will sometimes get it wrong and children and parents are quick to challenge if they feel an injustice. If diplomatic intervention by your (pastoral) deputy doesn't sort it out, then it is likely to end up on your desk. And things can quickly escalate unnecessarily if you don't take the time and trouble to gather all the facts carefully and even-handedly. So don't be rushed; but give all the parties concerned a realistic timescale for resolving matters, informed by your complaints policy.

Perhaps one of the most visceral pastoral judgments a school leader is called upon to make is when to exclude a student either for a short period of time or permanently. In either case, the situation may not be entirely clear cut, especially if it's one student's word against another. You'll have to exercise careful judgement, often informed by the balance of probabilities. And you're bound to feel privately that you/the school have failed the student in some way, so you have to be sure that what you are doing is, the long run, in the best interests of the student and, crucially, those around them, however grim it may seem at the time. Along with a careful rehearsal of the facts, that's a key message to get out to understandably aggrieved parents. And don't forget you can take advice from wise members of the school board (and certainly inform the chair), who will then give you support in the event of your judgment being challenged. Make sure you take proper legal advice too.

It's a fact of running a school that you'll spend a fair proportion of your time trying to resolve problems. Sometimes it can seem as if you only see the worst side of school life. So it's important to remember that the vast majority of students get on with what they have to do very happily and successfully. As head or principal, you are entitled to a share in that. So, why not have a regular slot in the week to meet students who have achieved commendations/done an especially good piece of work/have had an excellent report? And staff meetings should be an opportunity not only for raising students who are a cause for concern, but also to hear about excellent achievements. Make the most of your visits to classrooms too, or take a turn at a duty in the school yard to restore your sense of perspective and why you're doing one of the best of jobs: helping the next generation to get to grips with the complexities of the world around them.

******

Tom Gradgrind is in his fourth week as head of Fawcett's Academy (a secondary school of 1,000 students) when his pastoral deputy reports that a Year 11 boy is accused of repeatedly taunting and bullying another boy in his year group. A fight between the two boys has ensued which results in the alleged bully losing two front teeth and the other dislocating his jaw. They have both currently been kept at home by parents. Following discussions with the pastoral deputy, parents of the boy who has allegedly been bullied are demanding the permanent exclusion of the bully, but this is something the parents of the alleged bully will not accept, given the physical injury to their son. The pastoral deputy has referred the matter to Tom.

Tom decides to take the following actions:

- *Make sure he is totally familiar with the school's sanctions policy.*

- *Get a full written report on the incident from the pastoral deputy and records of any previously logged bullying incidents and any written witness statements.*
- *Inform the chair of the school board of a serious incident and steps he proposes to take.*
- *Consult with the safeguarding lead and take some legal advice*
- *Inform the school's insurers of the possibility of a claim.*
- *Interview each of the boys and parents involved with a view to showing he understands exactly what psychological/physical injuries have been sustained and what the longer term and short-term catalysts were to this incident.*

Following these actions, it becomes clear that:

- *There is little written evidence of previous bullying incidents and these have only just been reported by the boy and his parents, although on reflection some teachers have sensed ongoing antagonism between the two boys stemming from taunting from one boy about the other's lack of skill in sport.*
- *Both parents believe their son to be an equally injured party and neither set of parents will back down from their position on exclusion.*

In conclusion, Tom decides:

- *That, on the balance of probability and with further evidence from teaching staff, one boy has been the subject of some taunting by the other, leading to the current fight and thus deserves a harsher punishment than the other.*
- *That no physical violence can be excused, however provoked.*
- *Therefore, that both boys will be excluded for a fixed period, following the school's sanctions policy, with a slightly longer period for the boy who instigated the taunting.*
- *Re-admission to the school will be subject to a contract for good behaviour.*
- *He will explain the detail of his reasoning in person to parents and parents will be advised of the right of appeal to a panel of governors.*
- *Teachers will be told to keep a closer eye on potential bullying and that any concerns must be logged on the pastoral deputy's bullying log.*

Chapter 3
Teachers

Recruitment and selection. Setting expectations. Managing and appraising. Professional development. Some staff room stereotypes.

Although, as Winston Churchill once remarked, 'Heads have powers at their disposal with which Prime Ministers have never yet been invested', you'd be foolish to think you can achieve all you want by your own efforts alone. Schools must be one of a few places of work where the people you are leading have a good deal of day-to-day autonomy and where much of their work cannot (and should not) be micro-managed by senior leaders. So, of course, the professional quality of your teachers is vital. You'll want to have the very best possible team in place. And perhaps, here, the word *possible* needs further comment. There will, inevitably, be all sorts of constraints in the recruitment and deployment of teachers in your school: you'll never have the perfect team. Don't be frustrated by this: the challenge over time is to get the majority of colleagues to share your vision and manage those who won't or can't.

It's often the case that when a new head or principal is appointed some teachers decide this is a time for them to move on too. It's not necessarily that they don't like the look of you, but a change in leadership can make teachers reflect on their own career possibilities and priorities. So, this isn't necessarily a bad thing and does mean you have the opportunity to make some early appointments of your own. A thoughtful predecessor will want to get you involved in the recruitment and interview process in the couple of terms before you take over officially. Although this can seem as if you are trying to do two jobs at once, the investment of time in selecting the people with whom you are going to work in the coming years is well worth it. Appointing staff, and indeed developing their careers, is one of the most important things you'll do.

You'll know from your previous senior team involvement that there's an optimum 'hunting season' for teacher recruitment. In the UK, February/March time is probably the best time to advertise for an appointment for the following September. Teachers may be contemplating a change of scene or promotion as they begin to contemplate the following academic year. Furthermore, it means you can get the process done in time for teachers to give adequate notice to their current school (a term is often the norm in independent/private schools; half a term in the maintained/public sector). However, in many cases, you'll not to have the luxury of knowing a teacher is leaving until later in the term; or some jobs will start in January; or a maternity, paternity or adoption cover will be needed at some other point in the year. You just have to work out an advertising and interview schedule as quickly as possible and, if you're willing to put in temporary cover to get the right person in the long run, indicate that you're flexible about a starting date.

Whilst, in the UK, the TES seems pretty much still to have an (expensive) monopoly on advertising, don't forget to put the word around local contacts too. In a large school with an HR department, much of this will be taken care of for you. But it's still important that you push the process along and ensure the advertising material, and the process itself, reflects what you want to portray about the school to prospective applicants; and that the application form includes all the proper requirements for safeguarding declarations and employment checks. These days teachers, not schools, tend to command the buyers' market. Some schools now not only set out the job specification, salary, and material benefits, but also mention some of the 'fuzzier' benefits: friendly staff; refurbished classrooms; leafy surroundings. And with a bit of deft IT work, it's easy to include photos of smiling students in information packs. Also, remember that your website will get a large spike from prospective applicants, so make sure it's right up-to-date and does the job for them as well as for the more obvious constituents.

Once the application forms come in, whether to the HR department or to your office, check that you're happy with the way they are stored and acknowledged. The way in which applicants are treated from the start, even if they're eventually unsuccessful, can pay dividends for the reputation of your school in the local and wider community. Reading through applications is a time-consuming business and you'll have to decide whether or not you want to let a trusted senior colleague do a first trawl. Or you may want to sit down for an hour or two with a senior colleague and compare notes on each application. In any case, the second or even third opinion is worth having. If it's a junior job in a department or faculty, certainly involve the head of department. If it's an SLT appointment, involve a member of the school board. But remember you make the final decisions, unless it is specifically a trustee/governor appointment. Make sure you keep notes on each application so that if challenged (a not uncommon occurrence these days) about a decision not to interview, you have a clear view about a candidate's relative strengths and weaknesses for the post, in comparison with others you are interviewing.

Interview days should be fun. There's a sense of new possibilities and it's always a privilege to meet teachers from other schools, or fresh from training, all with new insights and ideas. It's one of those rarer days in a principal's or head's life when you get to discuss the craft of teaching, which is always energising and refreshing. You'll have prepared a list of questions for the interview and discussed/divided them up with your fellow interviewer(s). You should always have at least one other senior member of staff with you, or a trustee if staff are not available. Apart from corroborating what you say if the process is challenged at a later date, it's useful to spread the questioning so that you can observe the candidate while they are being questioned by others. And, of course, in the interests of equality, try to keep a proper gender/cultural balance on all interviewing panels.

A lesson observation is a 'must' and often a crucial decider in making an appointment. So, whilst the logistics of an interview day mean it's likely you'll not be able to observe lessons yourself, you need to make sure that the senior colleague who does has a clear grasp of what you/the school needs to see happening in a lesson. You can, of course, discuss plans for the lesson/how the lesson went in your interview session. This, plus what questions a candidate asks in advance about the lesson (e.g. How many SEND/additional needs pupils? What's the approximate ability range? What IT facilities are there?) will also tell you quite a bit about their teaching skills and habitual classroom methodology. Some schools also arrange tours with students: another very good way to find out how candidates interact in less formal situations. Your students will tell you exactly what they think and are often very shrewd judges of character!

It can be a terrible let-down at the end of an interview day when you've a growing realisation that no one you've seen really fits the bill. First of all, you should never worry about keeping the one or two better candidates courteously in the frame, explaining that you're going to have further interviews, but hope they will keep their hats in the ring. A second trawl, if you have time on your side, can often produce more candidates as people's circumstances change. However, as mentioned earlier, you may be in a situation where you are constrained to make an appointment fairly rapidly and you haven't much choice. In which case, trust your instinct about which of the candidates would cover things adequately and consider what in-school training you could put in place to support them. And keep in the back of your mind that, if the worse comes to the worst, all contracts have a probationary period.

But a good proportion of your interview days will end happily with a clear winner, endorsed by all involved in the process. And often a runner-up, too, who would be an asset. So, once the decision is made, it's good idea to phone the preferred candidate that very same evening, give them the good news, give a short time-frame for a decision, during which you will confirm the offer in writing, and get an instant reaction. Instant enthusiasm is balm; but if the vibes are lukewarm, it's not necessarily a downer, but you'll want to be on your guard and keep the runner-up on side.

As mentioned earlier, good teachers prize their autonomy in the classroom, but there is a fine line between that and the sort of protectionism which can mask complacent or lazy teaching. You'll need to make sure there are agreed policies and procedures in place for monitoring that teaching and learning are of the highest standards. But first of all, it's only fair to set out your general expectations of what needs to be done to continue to develop and maintain excellence in teaching and learning. You need to communicate this very clearly at the start of your tenure, at regular intervals thereafter, and then make sure it is enshrined in the staff handbook.

A good deal of it ought not to be news to your colleagues, but simply insisting on, for example, centrally-logged and up-to-date planning, bright and tidy classrooms, agreed procedures for the orderly start of lessons and moving around the school, timely feedback and formative marking, can set important benchmarks which will help you manage your teaching colleagues. There's a good deal to be said for focusing on particular expectations or targets for the whole teaching body each term, thus building up a collective culture of best practice as the year goes on. And bear in mind the now familiar SMART acronym[1] as a means to measure and check that your expectations can and are being met.

The school ought to have a system of appraisal, variously also known as performance management or professional development. Whatever the name, the object is the same: first, to endorse and commend what teachers have done well (who doesn't like a bit of praise?) and second, to identify areas for development or improvement, again bearing the SMART acronym in mind. It's pretty much essential to do this in some way or another on an annual basis. In a large school, you will have to delegate much or all of the process in some years to senior colleagues. But make sure you see the results and certainly see all staff yourself at least every two or three years. In a small school, an annual performance management discussion with all colleagues should be one of your diary priorities. Some (the best?) teachers will use this as a chance to discuss a new initiative or challenge; others will need a bit more prodding to come up with appropriate targets. And with some you may already have a clear idea of how shortcomings should be addressed: you will need to be very direct about what needs to be done to improve, how it is to be monitored, and over what timescale. That is only fair and, in most cases after the initial defensiveness, leads to a constructive dialogue and a willingness to do better.

---

[1] *Specific* – target a specific area for improvement.
Measurable – quantify or at least suggest an indicator of progress.
Assignable – specify who will do it.
Realistic – state what results can realistically be achieved.
Time-related – specify when the result(s) can be achieved.

However, demonstrable and repeated failure to meet your reasonable targets, and follow consistently applied policies on professional conduct, will almost certainly result in disciplinary action and you should then be scrupulous in following the school's policies in applying disciplinary measures, consulting lawyers if necessary. And if you do get to this stage after successive performance management conversations, it's more than likely that the individual concerned is fundamentally unhappy in their job, so a parting of the ways, however immediately disruptive, is probably a good outcome for all involved.

There are, sadly, occasional times when managing your team requires instant dismissal for serious professional misconduct. Here, make sure you act swiftly upon incontrovertible evidence, take legal advice and keep the chair of your school board fully informed. The boat will rock momentarily, but as long as you are sure of your facts and motives, decisive action is in the best interests of the school and students.

Much of the management of a group of teachers, however, is more informal. As in any organisation, successful management often revolves around the day-to-day quality of professional relationships between individuals. It doesn't take much always to have a cheerful word to say to everyone in the organisation and to remember and take an interest in their area of work or to send a brief note of appreciation (*handwritten* is especially good) for particular successes or initiatives. On a more personal level, it's good to have a system to remember people's birthdays with a card, for example, or remember something they've told you about their family. Equally, you shouldn't be afraid of having an informal professional discussion if you wish to get across an idea or a way of doing things. Tactfully sounding out colleagues over coffee or over lunch and asking for their input often helps to smooth the way for future development. Such strategies also help to keep up team morale which can flag particularly towards the end of a busy term. And as has been noted elsewhere, you're the one who has to keep on smiling even if the going is tough. You're the one who has to keep on saying (and believing) there are brighter times around the corner.

Professional development is important in any job if a workforce is to keep fresh and fully engaged. It will generally fall into three categories. First, to equip a member of staff with specific skills to undertake a new role. Second, to update skills for long-standing employees. Third, to assist employees in meeting agreed targets for improvement. For teachers, days away for professional development are often a bit more difficult to arrange than in other workplaces. There's always a concern to make sure courses are going to be relevant and value for money, and conscientious teachers will always worry about missing their classes and the additional costs to the school for supply teachers. (The reverse of this is that you have to guard against serial course attendees who are trying to escape the day job). It's a good idea to have a member of your senior team take specific charge of professional development, ranging from identifying and recommending useful courses, (perhaps prompted by you as a result of performance management conversations) to the nuts and bolts of facilitating cover for absence, monitoring frequency of attendance and then the quality of feedback into the overall school development plan. And don't neglect to encourage teachers to develop professional links with counterparts in other schools: one of the most cost-effective and productive ways of generating new ideas is to compare notes (with an agreed area of focus) with others doing a similar job in another setting.

Just as important as individual development is regular in-service training as a collective experience for the whole staff. This is especially helpful in bringing together classroom teachers with visiting music teachers or sports coaches. Diverse insights into teaching and learning are then shared to mutual benefit. It's all too easy for INSET days to be simply occasions for safeguarding and health and safety training with some administrative routines thrown in. Vital though these are, there's nothing like getting a really good speaker to shed new light on pedagogy or classroom management, according to the development priorities you have identified. That gets all staff animatedly discussing and reflecting on their practice and then sharing in-house wisdom. There's then a chance the momentum of the INSET day will roll on for a good few weeks into the term and begin to have a positive effect on teaching and learning across the school.

As a conclusion to this chapter, here are some thoughts on how to manage some of the types of colleagues you're likely to find in most school staffrooms in one way or another.

The ones who will be watching you most intently will be the long-serving members of staff who have carved out comfortable routines for themselves and are (like most people) wary of change. They usually divide into two categories: those who just want to keep under the radar and those who are disenchanted with teaching/the school/life in general who are active naysayers. The 'under-the-radar' merchants can usually be brought on board by a mixture of carrot and stick. A bit of informal checking-up by you or your senior team will probably get them to raise their game: they won't want to be under serious scrutiny (otherwise known as 'relentless support') for any length of time. Or judiciously getting them to lead on a new initiative (perhaps with the promise of a responsibility allowance if the budget will stretch to it) can reinvigorate a teacher who has simply slipped into routines by which even they are bored.

The naysayers are more problematic and potentially a corrosive influence as they sit in the staffroom and grumble to anyone who will listen. Nothing is going to be right with the world, let alone the school. Best to have an early conversation saying pretty directly that you've noticed their discontent and asking what can be done to help. Some will ask the immediately impossible (more promotion, more money, new classroom); some may allude to personal factors. Simply listening sympathetically can often help improve matters in the short term, but you have to start to have a plan to address their concerns. Perhaps promotion has to come in another school and maybe they need to work for a further qualification to achieve it; perhaps you need to point out that more money will require them taking on additional responsibilities; perhaps you could refurbish their classroom within a year or two. Or perhaps you need to consider what facilities there are in school to promote teachers' wellbeing in general. Does the counsellor see members of staff? Could you introduce mindfulness or yoga for staff? If there's nothing that will improve matters, then you might suggest they would be happier for a change of scene, first of course consulting the lawyers to make sure that you cannot be accused of constructive dismissal. And in all this, remember that one of the key underlying processes for effective management is to keep brief notes of all meetings with staff on file in case evidence is needed for any future actions.

The JAMS (just-about-managings) on your staff will essentially be grateful for your support. Characterised by an earnestness of purpose and a real vocational commitment to teaching, but ground-down by insecure discipline and unable by disposition to cut through the work efficiently, they are often stressed and stretched by their own conscientiousness. The best way you can help these sort of teachers is by showing that you recognise their qualities and have a non-judgemental discussion about how you can put in place strategies to help with discipline and workload. Showing the pupils that you have absolute solidarity with the teacher and lauding their expertise can have a very good effect on discipline, while gaining their confidence to get a senior member of your team to work with them on how to maximise planning, preparation and marking time can also help.

The bright and eager recent recruits to the staffroom will be your natural allies and are usually fairly low maintenance; but keep an eye that they don't take on too much and become disenchanted or worn out. The real godsends on your staff are those who have been in the place a while, but have constantly re-invented themselves and take on new ideas and challenges with measured professionalism. They often don't actively seek promotion, but if you can find ways of recognising their loyalty and commitment, perhaps by a bonus or support for a further qualification or training course, or simply a well-considered note of appreciation, then do so and they will continue to be outstanding colleagues for many years to come.

You'll notice, too, how in managing all these types, you come back yet again to the reason for doing all this in the first place: the education and wellbeing of the students. If any teachers appear to think they are in it for themselves – money, status, as part of a cosy club – then they will need your particular focus.

******

Anne Weston has been in post at Woodhouse School (an independent/private primary school of 300 students) for just over a year and has won the respect of students and parents for her thoughtful developments, which have brought about an improvement in teaching and learning standards as recognised in a recent inspection. Although all the staff pulled together for an inspection, several teachers have now slipped into less rigorous marking habits and have been the subject of parental complaints.

Anne decides to take the following actions:

- *Dedicate a staff meeting to the school's expectations of formative marking.*
- *Build upon on the inspection process and ask the academic deputy to start a weekly work scrutiny, looking at a selection of the exercise books of different subjects/year groups, focussing especially on books of teachers about whom complaints have been received.*
- *Feedback to teachers to be given by the academic deputy with constructive points for development.*

- *Develop the habit of students' own brief written feedback/strategies for improvement on each piece of work.*

In initiating these plans, she encounters the following reactions:

- *Books for scrutiny are pre-selected by teachers, so potential for unchecked patchy marking remains.*
- *The academic deputy reports that feedback to teachers and feedback from students need more consistent structure.*

Anne refines her plans:

- *By advising her academic deputy to call in fewer books and to select personally the books to be scrutinised.*
- *By making some timetable adjustments to enable the deputy to be free to do this efficiently.*
- *By asking the academic deputy to draw up a criterialed feedback form for teachers and students – the latter in consultation with heads of subject.*

Chapter 4
Senior Leadership Team

Deputy(ies). Size of the team. Job descriptions. Trust. Delegation

You will inherit a senior leadership team of one sort or another, which should include a designated deputy or two. They will be important eyes and ears around the place for you and will be confident and competent enough to take the reins when you are away from school, or if you are otherwise preoccupied on major school business. Deputies are often a crucial link between you and the staff; often teachers will confide in your deputies, who can be useful lightning conductors or temperature-takers in tricky times. If possible, it's helpful to get to know your immediate deputy both formally and informally before you start. Your professional relationship with them is going to be crucial and they have to understand from the outset that there will be developments and changes in which you will look to them to play their loyal part. Perhaps a meeting followed by a sociable drink, over which you listen to their take on how things are in the school. This could be a useful prelude to your first meeting with the wider senior team so that you have a little more background on key issues to discuss.

What you'll want to confirm straightaway, starting with your deputy, are the job descriptions and responsibilities of each member of the team. Crucially, are all the responsibilities for statutory and regulatory requirements properly represented or overseen in the senior team? Is each role within the team sufficiently defined? Are there unnecessary overlaps? What is the balance between academic and pastoral roles? Are all the key areas of school life properly represented according to its particular needs. For example, if the school has a particular strength in, say, sport or music, or additional needs, is that reflected in the skill set of the senior team? There's a lot in a name too. Do the job titles tell the wider world exactly what the roles cover?

Once you've done an audit of job descriptions, you may well want to begin to consider the size and shape of the team to ensure that collectively they are given scope to support you as effectively as possible. But, as mentioned in the first chapter, beware of making radical changes too early unless you feel the team is really not fit for purpose. As a new head or principal, you will really be out on your own if you do this: so be warned. If radical reshaping is called for, make sure you have the full backing of the governors for your changes and be aware of what additional responsibilities you may have to shoulder whilst the restructuring is taking place.

A lean team is probably best for most efficient day-to-day interaction, but many larger schools will have an additional tier of senior leadership, which often helpfully brings faculty heads or heads of year groups into the strategic running of the school. But beware of an overly large team which tends to send a detrimental subliminal message that those who are spending the majority of time in the classroom are somehow second-class citizens. And, by the same token, make sure that everyone in your team is a demonstrably excellent teacher and, wherever possible, takes their turn at cover and wider duties. By no means does every teacher have a talent for management, but your chosen managers *must* have a talent for teaching. It's probably obvious to say that if your school includes a junior school or a pre-prep or elementary school, then those in charge of these 'schools within schools', should certainly be on your senior team, the more crucially so if they are operating on a different site. You also need to make sure the support staff are represented by whoever is their overall manager: this is usually the finance officer or bursar who naturally will also have a useful financial voice in discussions.

Perhaps one of the perennial challenges for those running schools is to encourage everyone to do some strategic thinking at least at one or two junctures in the year. At the micro-level, this might entail a teacher re-assessing their planning to reflect pupils' changing needs. But it's important that members of your senior team think about developments at the macro-level and become creative and stimulating contributors to your thought-processes in drawing up, and regularly revising, the development and business plans. With the best will in the world, even senior leaders' thinking will still tend to be dominated for the most part by concern for their subject/pastoral area, rather than looking at issues from a whole school perspective. It's clearly important they bring the former to the SLT table, but it's the latter in which they'll need training and guidance from you (and perhaps a good external course too), especially if they are recent SLT appointees. This is particularly true of internal appointees who will be re-adjusting their strategic focus along with an initially uncomfortable need to manage colleagues with whom they had a different professional relationship in their previous role. Many schools have an awayday for the school board to chew over larger issues; why not extend this to include all members of the SLT? It's a good opportunity for them to meet trustees, and vice-versa, and you can develop their whole school thinking by getting them to present a paper on an aspect of their current development planning.

So, you've taken a view on individuals' strengths, made sure they are up to the job (getting rid of an inherited poor-performing SLT member requires especial care) and that their roles are well-defined and do-able. You're beginning to build up a sense of a team. You're beginning to feel it's not just you out on a limb anymore. And from this you build up mutual trust. As the American author Ernest Hemingway once put it: 'The best way to find out if you can trust somebody is to trust them.' Trust in your senior team can be shown in small but significant ways. Is your door/email always open to your SLT? In other words, show them that you trust them not to bother you with trivia, but equally to have the judgement to know when to pop in to give you support. Trust them with confidential information, provided you warn them it is confidential, so that you can discuss worries and concerns freely. Trust them enough to be yourself in SLT meetings. Whilst you need to retain your overall leadership qualities of resilience and decisiveness, don't be afraid to show your human side too. You ought to be able to trust your senior team enough to laugh and cry with them. And then, perhaps most importantly, you have to get to a point where mutual trust means they will tell you how it is. The old adage 'speak truth to power' is worth trotting out to your trusted colleagues from time to time. They need to be comfortable taking you out of your comfort zone and saying when they think you've got it wrong. You don't have to take their advice every time, but they may well have a perspective you've overlooked. And every time you give them credit for that, the mutual trust increases. In a really well-functioning SLT, nobody, not even the head or principal, should feel undermined for having their ideas raked over and refined. Collective wisdom is a real strength: everyone involved in running a school should have the confidence to see that.

You've got to the point, then, when you're comfortable with the close-knit team around you, but make sure that it isn't perceived by other employees to be disconnected from them. The nature of school teaching is that most employees will, rightly, spend most of their time interacting with their students. But they will also want the company of adults in the workplace: it's natural to want to discuss professional concerns, share chat, even confidences, with colleagues. And although it's more difficult for the principal or head to be part of that (often you are expected to keep your distance from the staff room), your SLT should make time for such conversation, perhaps in the staff room or at lunch, especially looking out for the people for whom they have immediate professional care.

Finally, the art of delegation to your SLT is perhaps one of the trickiest areas in which you'll have to translate fine theory into effective practice. As noted before in this chapter, you'll have defined responsibilities and job descriptions; but being certain you can delegate, knowing that decisions and judgements made by your SLT are not going to return to your desk, requires constant training, empowerment and a certain amount of gentle 'sink or swim'. If your SLT colleagues think they can always pass the buck to you, they'll never feel that sense of learning from their mistakes, or taking ultimate responsibility for their decisions, and your job will become unmanageable. Once you've delegated something, you want to be sure it is sorted. Your SLT colleagues will need to learn from you that their judgements will sometimes be questioned, that they will need to be resilient in the face of potential flak from colleagues and parents, but that you believe in their integrity to take the best course of action. And if they get into difficulties and make mistakes, you need to show you believe they can sort things out. That's the gentle 'sink or swim' approach.

But in a crisis, such as a major school incident or unexpected external events (who could have predicted a pandemic in which schools were forced to make major changes to their operation?) which pre-occupy you, your SLT may have to learn all this very quickly. It's amazing how human beings can rise to the challenge when under pressure. But it's a good idea for you to consider as part of a critical incident plan not only what key pieces of information you would give your team to keep things going in a crisis, but also what your headline statement would be to keep them all focussed and calm? Without being too dramatic about it, imagine what you would pithily say to them to ensure that the values and vision of the school continued to be led effectively, even as you were carried off to hospital on a stretcher. I hope it never happens to you, but it's worth a few moments' thought.

******

Charlie Mell has just taken over at Copperfield College (a secondary school of 1,000 students) and has inherited a large SLT with very generous timetable allowances. In an early conversation, the principal deputy expresses her frustration that Charlie's predecessor had allowed the SLT to grow to unmanageable proportions and SLT meetings have become fragmented and unproductive. The school has also had a budget cut because of a falling roll.

Charlie decides to take the following actions:

- *Ask the principal deputy for a list of timetable allowances for all staff with details of how and for what duties the allowances are awarded.*
- *Ask the Finance Office for details of financial allowances for all staff.*
- *Having obtained this information, carry out a comparative audit of staff timetable and financial allowances.*
- *Ask each member of the SLT to set out their current responsibilities and job descriptions, followed up with an individual conversation to discuss them.*
- *With governors' agreement, draw up a plan for the whole SLT to meet once a fortnight and a smaller 'head's advisory group' consisting of the head, the academic and pastoral deputies, and the bursar/finance officer to meet once a week to deal with ongoing matters and set clear agendas for the SLT meeting. Timetable and financial allowances will*

need to be adjusted accordingly and HR/lawyers consulted about proposed changes.

In taking these actions, Charlie encounters the following issues:

- *The timetable and financial allowances are inconsistent, even between members of the SLT doing similar roles.*
- *SLT members are anxious about setting out and discussing job descriptions and, in some cases, are even actively resistant to doing so. Others appear to have inflated the importance of small tasks.*
- *Some have got wind of the plan for a 'head's advisory group' and start openly criticising the work of the deputies.*

Charlie attempts to resolve these issues by:

- *Working confidentially with the finance officer/bursar (advised by HR/lawyers) to draw up a consistent blueprint for timetable and financial allowances for all staff to be phased in as roles change and vacancies occur. Some redundancies may have to be made to meet the reduced school budget. Charlie will have to be careful about how and when these plans are announced.*
- *Being clear about the need to review the operation of the SLT so that colleagues' time is not wasted by inefficient meetings.*

- *Sharing details of the school's budget in confidence with the SLT, and the need to make economies.*
- *Setting deadlines for job description reviews and challenging inefficiencies in duties and roles.*
- *Quietly warning those criticising the deputies that he has full confidence in the deputies' work and reassuring them that the proposed revised pattern of leadership meetings means all voices are more likely to be heard more effectively.*

Chapter 5
The School Board

Defining their role. Good communications. Formal structures. Know the characters. Using skill sets. Parent-trustees. Managing factions. The clerk to the school board. Mutual respect.

It goes without saying that the relationship between you and your school board is vital. But the relationship is a delicate one and a good number of leadership roles have foundered on poor trustee/principal/head relations. Objectively speaking, their role is an important check and balance on your considerable powers and so you should not resent their enquiries although, equally, they should be aware of their boundaries. It's an old adage that school leaders get the school boards they deserve, so you need to get to know the individuals and work out how best they can support you, starting crucially with the chair. The good news is that they have backed you for the job. They want you to succeed and will be keen to back you for a flying start. So, as recommended in the first chapter, take time early on – even before you're in post – to confirm what their vision for the school is over the next few years and begin to sketch out how your vision (after all, you are the executive professional) and theirs will coincide to take the school forward. Albeit with a bit of tweaking, coincide they must or trouble lies in store.

Ultimately trustees have to take responsibility for whatever strategic development takes place so, both in good times and bad, supportive members of the school board are invaluable and mutual trust is important. The best are 'critical friends', knowing that they are not running the place, but willing to offer advice if asked, willing to raise questions if they think things are going wrong, and willing to get stuck in to solve problems if needed. Most school boards will consist of a range of people who have expertise in their own fields and so, apart from their formal oversight, they will be good informal and confidential sounding boards on a range of issues. So consult them early; don't battle on by yourself.

All this presupposes transparency and good communication between you and the school board. There might be a few issues which remain confidential to you and the chair, but generally speaking it's best to keep all informed and involved as much as possible. Your reports to board meetings should be full and informative, ranging widely over the activity of the school and commenting frankly on teaching and learning, pastoral matters, staffing, finance, recruitment and retention of students, responses to statutory requirements and *always* reporting on safeguarding and health and safety. Your first report will set the tone and the form for the future. So, before you write your first report, check-in with the chair that you are covering the areas which the board expects to hear about or about which they have particular immediate concerns. You should invite trustees to visit the school to see it in action in the classroom and not just on state occasions (although their presence at these events is a useful signal to parents of the board's support and interest). Members of the board should also be called upon to sit on interview panels for senior staff appointments: for this, you'll need to make sure they have had training in safe recruitment of staff. And why not get heads of department to present short papers on their work at one or two board meetings a year? Good for teachers, good for members of the board. And are trustees on your school mailing list for newsletters and the like? They can always tell you if they have information overload, but better that way round than a feeling of being kept at arms' length.

The formal board structure will, of course, be the basis for the flow of information and it's best to take an early view on how these structures work in practice. Is there a regular meeting/phone call with the chair which allows you and them to raise routine matters arising? Are there sub-committees? Too few or too many? Are their distinctive functions sufficiently well-defined? Do they all have equal importance, or is everything wrapped up in something like a Finance and General Purposes Committee? Is there an overview of trustees' skill sets and how those are matched to specific roles (e.g. safeguarding, health and safety) or relevant sub-committees? For how long do members of the board serve and how is succession-planning managed? How is the chair selected/elected? Whilst this is not part of your remit to direct, it's useful to keep an eye on things and ask questions at the right moment.

Above all, you need to be alert for well-intentioned attempts at micro-management by trustees. As mentioned above, they are primarily there to ask questions, to be sounding boards for advice and to give a steer on strategic direction. They have selected you to lead and manage the school on a daily basis, so be diplomatically clear about boundaries. You'll soon get to know the individual characters and the best ways in which they can help you and the ways in which they might overstep the mark.

Retired or serving heads or principals are often very wise, experienced, counsellors and will be advocates to other members of the board of the human complexities of running an educational institution. With a first-hand understanding of children's needs, they are good people to have trustee responsibility for safeguarding. But beware the principal or head who would really like to be running your school without taking day-to-day responsibility.

Most school boards will have members with a background in finance or business: their business know-how will be invaluable in helping you to make the most of your resources, but just because they've allocated so many thousands to the IT budget doesn't necessarily mean they can expect the public exam results to improve commensurately. Lawyers are another group often well-represented on school boards: they are good at reading all the meeting papers thoroughly and asking forensic questions, which can be very useful in discovering potential flaws in plans and ideas. What you can't do is ask them for free legal advice. No lawyer worth their salt would do that and, although they are invaluable in giving a general steer about overall process, you'll need to consult the school's paid lawyers or your local or professional association's lawyers who are indemnified in case they give the wrong advice.

Other useful skills amongst your board might be an architect or someone with building/planning expertise, someone with a personnel/HR background, a medic, an academic or perhaps a local councillor or two. All these will help you to a better understanding of relatively specialist areas which principals and heads are frequently called upon to deal with. If you have a building project going on, for example, chances are you'll have to get up to speed with a lot of new terminology and processes. A bit of 'on-side' trustee expertise will save you a lot of time and angst, but it cannot be allowed to take the place of the paid professional work.

Some schools, especially schools with a religious or similar institutional affiliation, will have trustees appointed by the foundation. These trustees, of course, have a duty to your school, but they also represent the interests of the overarching foundation. Whilst in most cases this is likely to be chiefly about maintaining values and ethos, you need to be alert for potential conflicts of interest which might be detrimental to the school, and not be afraid to flag them up pretty clearly in meetings if necessary.

Of all the school board characters, the former pupil and the current/former parent need particular attention. These are obvious candidates for membership of the school board because they care deeply about the school and often want to 'give something back' in gratitude for a positive school experience. So their motivation is strong and genuine. Former pupils are an excellent link with the wider community and may well be useful in helping with fundraising. Their disadvantage is that they may not see the need for change and development and may have a sentimental view of the school's past. Of course, it depends on disposition and outlook, so try to make sure the board selects with care. Ditto the parent-trustee. Their immediate and first-hand knowledge of the school, and their contact with other parents, can be a real asset in helping you to judge how the school's strengths and weaknesses are perceived and what the chatter is on social media. Although confidential and full of integrity most of the time, even the most conscientious parent-trustee has a weak spot when it comes to airing issues which affect their own child. You really don't want meetings side-tracked by questions about the Science homework in Year 9 or misbehaviour at the local bus stop, based on their child's observations. That's the moment for the chair to come to your rescue or, if the issue gets a head of steam from others on the school board, you have to step in and say you'll ask the relevant colleagues to investigate the specific concerns of the parent-trustee and then report back to the whole board if these are part of a bigger picture. Again, the message is clear: trustees should be guided away from micro-management. Perhaps the best parent-trustees are parents whose children have recently left the school. They combine all the practicality of first-hand knowledge and love of the school without the personal baggage. And their sense of perspective might well be salutary to the over-enthusiastic current parent.

Alas, some boards are prone to develop factions. Whilst it is the role of the board to express views trenchantly and engender lively and worthwhile discussion, sometimes opinion can divide between the 'hawks' and the 'doves'. This is a dangerous moment for the principal/head, especially if the chair finds themselves dragged onto one side or the other. You will know that running a school is a subtle business and that what might seem to the board to be quick and simple solutions aren't going to work in your set up. With the help of the chair, you'll need to try to bring opposing views together by providing a tenable executive compromise which all parties can sign up to. You'll have to work hard at putting the arguments and especially working hard with the opinion-formers. Otherwise, you risk being caught in the cross-fire, with a commensurate loss of the board's trust in you. This can snowball very quickly with potentially disastrous professional consequences for you.

The role of clerk to the school board varies from school to school, but you need to make sure you understand their particular remit. The clerk fulfils an important administrative function in setting up meetings and taking minutes. The quality of minute-taking is crucial to the equitable functioning of the board and you will need to take an informal check early on that all opinions are adequately reflected, especially if there are likely to be the sort of factions referred to above. It's likely that the clerk will have another role within the school, often that of bursar, finance officer or office manager. Even if only informally, they will bring their perspective on school life and may be quietly sounded out by trustees from time to time, so it's sensible to make sure they have an appropriate and confidential understanding of key developments and issues, in advance of meetings, to avoid any misunderstandings.

It's probably quite surprising to a new principal or head how much trustees need to be guided and indeed should be encouraged to go on training/information courses as appropriate. That's not to say that they are devoid of their own ideas – in fact quite the reverse – but they are often busy professionals with their own day-to-day concerns. So, in summing up this chapter, it's important to stress again how much trustees are reliant upon your openness about what is going on in the school and, therefore, your need to keep the communication flowing. Err on the side of caution. If in doubt, pick up the phone or email the chair and share information. They will know their fellow board members well enough to advise you wisely if an FYI email to all is a good idea. And perhaps rather obvious to say, they are reliant on your educational expertise, so don't be afraid, if necessary, to assert that you're the expert when it comes to the fundamentals of teaching and learning. Members of the board will respect you for it, just as you will be careful to respect their areas of expertise. And with that, you should have the school board you deserve.

******

Bertha Flowers was an internal appointment as principal at Washington High School (an 11–18 secondary school) having previously been the school's pastoral deputy. The chair of the school board is a former parent whose children Bertha taught a few years ago. Bertha is pleased to be working with someone who is very pro-active and whom she knows and trusts. However, after the first two board meetings, Bertha sees that other trustees have very little input and meetings are dominated by the chair.

Bertha decides to take the following actions:

- *Send a personal invitation to each member of the board to come into school to see some classes in action and meet her over coffee/tea so she can build up a good working relationship with all trustees.*

- *Draw up a plan to give more members of the board specific responsibilities e.g. interest in/oversight of safeguarding, risk assessment, curriculum, the arts, sport, and report back at meetings.*
- *With the co-operation of the chair, sound out potential trustees among alumni/parent/the local community with a view to moving on those who will find more active input too time-consuming.*
- *Ask heads of department to give presentations at board meetings, so all members of the board are more familiar to staff.*

She encounters the following difficulties:

- *A large number of trustees say they cannot come in during the school day because of work commitments.*
- *The chair expresses reservations about other members of the board taking on specific roles, saying that the previous head always felt she carried out all oversight very effectively and it was the most efficient way of maintaining strong communication between the board and the head.*
- *After sounding out potential trustees, the interest is overwhelmingly from current parents and few others.*

She resolves to:

- *Extend invitations to come in and meet her in the later afternoon/early evening so that she can still discuss their role, even if they do not see the school in action.*

- *Be direct with the chair about the need for changes to make best use of all trustees' talents and make sure others are aware of training opportunities which would empower them in their role.*
- *Talk to local businesses/institutions (e.g. law firms, accountancy firms, architects' practices, hospitals, places of worship, other schools) to see if they might suggest potential candidates for board membership.*

Chapter 6
Parents and Carers

Partnership with parents and carers. Cultivating good relationships. Communications. Parents and grandparents as allies. Managing expectations and being proactive about perennial niggles. Some types of parent and how to manage them. Being responsive and alert to escalation. Policies and legal advice to ensure events don't overtake you. The silent majority.

One of the healthier developments in educational theory and practice in recent decades has been the way in which schools and governments have encouraged much greater involvement of parents and carers in their children's education. Until the latter half of the twentieth century there were no league tables, end-of-term reports were often terse, sometimes eccentric, and parent/teacher contact was minimal beyond a few parent-teacher social events. However much, as principal or head, you may occasionally find contact with over-zealous parents irksome, we all know that well-judged parental support and involvement in a child's education are vital to that child's wellbeing and progress. Schools are privileged to be entrusted with other people's children – the most precious beings in the world to a parent – and our starting point with parents should be about respecting that trust.

In the first chapter, I mentioned a few ways in which you could quickly make yourself known to parents, but cultivating good relationships and partnership with parents and carers is an ongoing process in which you must take a strong lead. First, you'll need to make sure that parents and carers have easy ways of communicating with the school, whilst making sure that you put reasonable boundaries in place to protect you and your colleagues from a constant deluge of emails or text messages. What is your school's email/mobile phone policy? Are staff email addresses advertised to parents? How quickly should you/your staff be expected to reply? As a rule of thumb, it's best gently to remind parents that teachers can't be expected to reply to emails during the school day because they are teaching! But, equally, teachers may need to be reminded that replies after/before school, as part of the normal working day, are expected. Most schools now use social media or text alerts to keep parents informed: you'll need to consider how this burgeoning area of communication is managed in a way which reflects your school's priorities and style and avoids duplication or error.

In your own communications, you'll need to decide whether your emails come to you via your PA or whether you would prefer to deal with them directly. And always consider when it might be best to phone parents to discuss something rather than have an endless back and forth of emails. Whatever policy you adopt, frame it in such a way as to encourage measured and informed communication, rather than looking defensive. And set out your policy clearly as soon as you can to avoid unmanageable expectations taking root.

The same applies to parents and carers visiting the school: you need to be clear what the ground-rules are going to be. Whilst your safeguarding policy will clearly preclude any visitors from wandering around the school unsupervised or unannounced, it's important to make parents feel welcome. How are parents greeted by the office staff? How easily can they get appointments to see you or your colleagues? Are you able to have a reasonably 'open-door' to see parents? Do you encourage parents to come into school to hear reading with younger students, or to talk about their jobs as part of careers education for older students? Could you invite parents to assemblies from time to time, and not just the big shows/concerts? How easy is it for them to get to sports matches? Would it be supportive to children and teachers to allow parents of younger students to sit in on 1:1 music lessons or learning support sessions? Carefully reviewing all these policies and practices will send signals to parents that you welcome their involvement and want a positive and productive partnership with them.

It's wise to take a good look at the structure of the formal processes of communication with parents and carers and make a judgement about just how user-friendly they are. Busy parents will not thank you for inefficient or cumbersome arrangements which do not show an understanding of the complexities of family life. Make sure your website has an easily-accessible parents' portal, but equally, remember that parents appreciate being updated with immediately relevant information in a regular newsletter, and/or on social media, or even by text alerts. And how do you make sure you engage with parental concerns or interests in what you send out? Does the school, for instance, share an overview of schemes of work with parents? Many schools issue a parents' handbook at the start of the year. Not only, of course, will you want to check its accuracy, but some reflection on how the information is set out, ensuring rapid access to key information, will surely be appreciated by parents.

You'll want to scrutinise the schedule for reports and parents' evenings too. Often there will have been an accretion of these as schools have sought to become more accountable. But obviously, quality and timing are prime considerations for parents. Reports should give an informative judgment about a child's progress with strategies for development, so it's time for reform if they are simply a summary of the work covered. Does the grade/mark/percentage system give parents an intelligible objective view of their child's performance? How often are reports issued? And at what points in the school year? Are the timings designed for the convenience of the school or with consideration of parents in mind? For instance, some schools have a habit of issuing reports at or after the end of term, leaving much less opportunity for feedback and discussion. Not the best way of cultivating partnership with parents and often leaving questions to fester dangerously over a school holiday. Parents' evenings can also become potential sources of irritation too. Whilst there will be pressure from your teaching colleagues to start promptly in the late afternoon/early evening, family and work commitments for parents may make this a difficult time, so again flexibility and understanding of this will be appreciated. Could you provide extended after-school care for younger students? And what is your policy about older students attending with parents? And how do you make best provision for parents of boarders from overseas who may only visit once or twice a year? Are you making use of videoconferencing facilities? Lastly, on parents' evenings, do what you can to alleviate the perennial discontent over appointment systems, which never seem to work. In small schools, you might be able to get rid of appointments altogether and allow parents to circulate at choice with all the teachers gathered together in the school hall. In larger schools, you might limit the number of teachers that parents can book to see. And small gestures, like providing refreshments, will go a long way to building up goodwill and a feeling of welcome.

That feeling of welcome and goodwill will spread far too. As will be seen in chapter eight, you will want to establish the school's good reputation in the community. Parents have more choice than ever now. The 'word on the street' (or more likely on social media) will be vital in promoting your school's particular qualities. And don't forget grandparents in all this. Many grandparents are part-time carers for younger children (perhaps subsidising fees in independent/private schools) and, with fewer other demands on their time, particularly enjoy being part of the school community. They often have a greater sense of perspective when it comes to those little irritants of school life. They've seen it all before and are generally under no illusions about their grandchildren's strengths and weaknesses: useful support to you if parental perspective gets too narrow. So, make sure you know and include grandparents or other significant seniors in your planning for community events and, chances are, they will be some of your staunchest allies.

However good your school is, and however attentive you are to parents, there are always going to be perennial niggles, usually revolving around uniform, parking, food, or lack of information. But with a certain amount of proactivity and skill in managing expectations, you should be able to keep these under control. And the power of an apology should never be underestimated. If you or one of your colleagues has made a forgivable error, then you shouldn't hesitate to say sorry and do your best to rectify the situation. The empathy and humility this shows will win the respect of most parents and enable everyone to move on with honour satisfied.

Another way in which you can be proactive with parents is to have a regular parents' forum at which you invite parents and carers to discuss issues which concern them. Or you could do this in a more streamlined way through a committee of class representatives. Although this can sometimes be an opportunity for more vocal parents to air grievances, rather than a representative majority, it's another good way of finding out what parents are worrying about. Often worries are to do with the perennial niggles mentioned above and are pretty easy to fix. You'll quickly find, too, that if one or two parents hog the floor, others will step in and put them right. But above all, you will be appreciated for your openness in letting people have their say.

Parents, of course, are as infinite in their variety as their children. But as one wise school leader once put it: 'To meet the parents is to understand everything about the children.' So here's a guide to some of the characters who you might typically find in your school and how you might work with them to the benefit of their children. And do remember that nearly all parents have moments of anxiety about their children – it's a natural part of parenting – and a good deal of that anxiety can show itself in the way they deal with you and the school. Without being too much of an amateur psychologist, part of your job is to try to understand the root of these anxieties and how they manifest themselves in all sorts of different ways in all sorts of different people.

Perhaps one of the more obvious anxieties comes from dual-working parents who have delegated the care of younger children to grandparents, neighbours, nannies or the like or who simply haven't had enough time, for example, to keep an eye on their teenager who is now in trouble for sending offensive images to other pupils on their phone. Most of the time, you hardly ever hear from these parents, but when difficulties loom or a report sounds a loud wake-up call, they rush into school demanding immediate action to put things right, part of which is to do with their own sudden feelings of guilt. For the most part, they have not been inherently neglectful and things might have turned out in the same way had they been totally in charge. But you need to take a step back and remind yourself what lies behind their demands and reassure them appropriately.

The opposite of these sorts of parents is the so-called 'helicopter parent' who will be on their child's case (and probably yours as well) almost every day. What you need to remember about these parents is that whilst they may take up a disproportionate amount of your time, which is unfair on all the other people who have an equal call on you, they are also not helping their children to develop as independent learners who should be starting to take some practical and emotional responsibilities for themselves. That's primarily what you need to tackle. One way of doing this is to bring the student in to hear appropriate parts of discussions you or your colleagues have with parents. Give the student space to ensure their voice and opinions are heard and you then have some chance of bringing about a better balance in the parent/child relationship, at least where school matters are concerned.

Then there are some parents for whom nothing is ever quite right. They are not inherently negative, but they seem to seek for a school in which everything is perfectly aligned for their own child's needs. That's never going to happen because a school is a community in which people have to make compromises to co-exist, and judgements have to be made: that's part of the educational journey. So, these parents are the first to want their child to be in a different class from the one allocated, or to be in a different sports team, or to be selected for a different part in the school play. In search of the perfect school, you might spot they have a track-record of taking their children in and out of different schools. Unless there is a serious, intractable problem, you'll do your best to explain it's unlikely the 'grass will be greener' elsewhere. But ultimately you may graciously have to let them move, whilst being professionally frank with them that serial school-changing is not going to be in their child's best interests.

Sadly, it's fair to say that in your time as head or principal you may have to deal with parents who are wildly irrational and/or simply dangerous. Here, for obvious reasons, the usual professional dialogues do not work. It's time for very blunt talking and protective measures; and you'll have to start invoking your school's code of conduct for parents and carers. Whilst walking away from a problem is not normally at all a proper response, you will sometimes have to decide that you have a serious confrontation on your hands which cannot be resolved by the normal reasonable channels of communication. And, unless you're an absolute saint, it's likely that you might lose your cool. So, it's time to say that the meeting/email exchange/phone call can go no further for the moment and call on your PA or another colleague to move the parent on and arrange another time for them to make their point. Sometimes, you will know that a parent's behaviour is the result of physical or mental illness and that discussion with another member of their family might help resolve the situation. In the most extreme cases of difficult parental behaviour, you'll certainly want to alert the chair of your school board. And you do have the power to ban a parent from entering the school premises, enforced by legal action if necessary. That may be necessary to protect not only you, but pupils and colleagues alike.

However, let me reassure you that if you build up good relationships, most parents will let the school get on with its job. But as noted at the start of this chapter, children are the most precious things in the world to parents and they will make their views felt if they feel their children have been poorly served. You'll need to make sure, in leading the school, that there's a culture of responsiveness in teacher and support staff communication with parents. Matters always fester and escalate if left, particularly now that the ease of email/text communication means that a prompt response is not unreasonable. As noted earlier on, you'll have put in place protocols for reply which mean that nobody's reply need be rushed or ill considered. But a holding email explaining that a matter is being considered will take away any initial sting, start to smooth the path to positive resolution, and will do its bit to support that inherently good relationship you have built up.

All schools are required to have a formal complaints policy and are required to send this to parents. This will usually provide for routine concerns/complaints to be resolved informally in the first instance, but for anything more serious or protracted, obviously you must follow the policy scrupulously. If you've got a sense that something is going to unravel big time, then make sure you keep your chair informed and take legal advice/advice from your professional association at an early opportunity so you don't make wrong moves and, crucially, you gain support for your strategy at an early stage rather than letting events overtake you.

In concluding this chapter, I want to focus again on the silent majority of parents who just let you get on with the job. These are the people you should always keep in mind when other voices seem louder. Just because they do not communicate regularly doesn't mean to say that they are not appreciative of what the school is doing or that they are not actively supporting their child, you, and the school in the community. But quite rightly they know you are busy, just as they are, and that superfluous comment is not helpful. These are the parents who may rarely be in contact, except for appreciative comments at parents' evenings, until they write the most touching card or letter when their child leaves the school, telling you how the school has helped their daughter or son to develop in ways you may never have thought. And, unless you're doing something very wrong, remember they *are* the majority.

******

Rick Braithwaite is head of Greenslade School, an urban primary school of 250 students. After an initial warm welcome from parents, he has noticed an increasing number of questioning emails and phone calls every time he begins to introduce even the smallest change or innovation. This is despite carefully flagging up the details and need for any such changes well in advance in a regular newsletter.

Rick decides to:

- *Talk through changes with the parents' association.*
- *Make sure that all teachers and support staff are clear in the way they communicate changes to parents.*
- *Send out a reminder of the detail of his plans just before they are introduced.*
- *Make a habit of being at the school gate at pick-up time to chat to parents and gauge responses to his changes.*

He encounters the following:

- *Some staff are opposed to his changes and are sharing their concerns with parents.*
- *A good number of parents never read his newsletters.*
- *Two or three parents are loudly spreading misinformation (either deliberately or through misunderstanding) at the school gate.*

To help resolve these, Rick:

- *Has a formal meeting with staff who have been sharing concerns with parents to ask them about their concerns and to underline the need for collective loyalty. He decides not to warn them yet that disciplinary action could follow if they persist, but makes a note of the meeting on file.*
- *Makes more use of social media in his communications with parents and reviews the presentation of his newsletter.*
- *Asks his deputy to engage the 'opinion-formers' at the school gate in conversation so they have less time to chat with other parents and so that any misinformation can be corrected.*

Chapter 7
Support Staff

Job descriptions. Business Manager/Bursar. Head's P.A. Admin team. HR. IT. Science technicians. Library. Catering. Caretaking/maintenance team. Developing efficiency.

Amongst the many less familiar roles you'll take up as a new principal or head is your overview and care for support staff. Whilst you may not be their immediate manager (this is usually a bursar's or school business manager's role), too often these are the unsung heroes of school life and one of your jobs is to make sure their work is recognised and celebrated by the whole community. Without their attention to the infrastructure of the school, it's not an exaggeration to say that what goes on in the classroom would quickly founder: teachers sometimes need to be reminded of that.

So, first of all, you'll need to make sure you know who does what job and make a point of meeting them informally on their territory and talking to them about what they do. It's important for team morale that you take an early interest in all that's going on. But you also need to have an informed view about how the various strands of support fit into the overall operation.

The bursar or school business manager is a member of the support staff with whom you'll work very closely and will often be part of your SLT. The relationship between you and your business manager/bursar is crucial. In controlling the purse-strings, managing the support team, directing building and maintenance projects, and often being in attendance at school board meetings, they are powerful figures. As such, too, they are a close and well-placed check and balance on your considerable powers. Often bringing experience from the world of business or from the military services, they are also sources of good strategic advice and can be great allies when knotty problems need to be solved. But there needs to be mutual understanding. A good business manager or bursar will make it their job to get to know what goes on in the classroom and understand your priorities for developing teaching and learning. Equally, you'll need to get to know how to read spreadsheets and financial projections and understand that the business manager's priorities lie in prudent housekeeping.

Heads and principals can be frustrated by the apparent default position of many bursars/business managers to pour cold water on initiatives which require substantial expenditure, but you need to remember that they are only doing their job of testing the cost-effectiveness of your proposals. You'll need to put forward your rationale with care and detail and prove this is a wise use of resources. If you can convince the business manager/bursar, it's likely you have put together a well-argued case which can be presented more widely. Although as head/principal you make the ultimate running, you're aiming for unanimity of vision and it's right and proper that this should be the product of robust collaboration and discussion.

Much of your day-to-day admin will be made so much easier by having a really good PA. You may have been used to working with some administrative support in a previous SLT role, but when you're in ultimate charge you will depend much more on your PA who will take a considerable lead in organising a large part of your life. They must be someone with whom you know you can freely share confidences: you will find such trust will be re-paid over and over again. Apart from their obvious administrative support in managing your diary, getting those emails and phone calls sorted, and taking minutes at senior meetings, they are your gate-keeper, your eyes and ears in the community and, above all, they will get to know your working habits and take the initiative to support them in all sorts of productive ways which you probably won't even be conscious of. In many instances, they will be one of the people who represent the public face of you and the school, so their tone on the phone, in emails and towards visitors to the school is vitally important. Keep an ear out to ensure that this is a good mixture of friendliness and efficiency.

Depending on the size of the school, your PA may well be in charge of/work with an office team giving administrative support to particular areas of the operation and/or to other members of staff. It makes for contented working if roles and responsibilities are well-defined and each member of the team has a clear sense of their particular expertise. But at pinch-points in the term, or in unexpected emergencies, you must encourage a culture of everyone pitching in together.

Apart from general administrative support, there are likely to be a number of specialist support departments for you to consider: examples will include IT (and just think how dependent on IT your school is!), library staff, science technicians, school medical staff and, in a large school, a human resources department. Support staff in these areas will be primarily interacting with teaching staff and some will be directly managed by them. As has been noted earlier, not all teachers make immediately good managers, so a little bit of training to ensure that working relationships are neither too casual nor too dictatorial will go a long way in getting the best from all involved. It's worth bearing in mind that in a small school, some of these could be 'departments' of one. Not having someone to compare notes with can be quite morale-sapping at times, so a bit of extra care from you will be especially appreciated.

As Napoleon is once reputed to have said, 'An army marches on its stomach.' Similarly, much of the wellbeing of the whole school community will hinge upon the quality of the catering department's operation. Without falling into the trap of micro-managing, you'll want to be alert to the potentially conflicting forces that can bedevil a school's catering operation. An obvious first question is whether the whole operation meets the school's needs best in-house, or whether it's better outsourced to a larger independent company. It's as well to remember that different sections of the community will have different dietary needs. I don't just mean that a school kitchen has to take account of religious and health requirements, but also that the eating preferences of members of staff are typically going to be different from growing adolescent students or small children in the youngest year groups. A good caterer has to balance all these needs against calls from the Finance Department (and indeed parents) to keep catering costs down. You could well find yourself arbitrating on what is best for the pupils, what is best for the school's/parents' finances and what is the art of the possible within an often-limited lunchtime. But as with all areas of school life, it's important to show that you care constructively about the quality of what goes on in the catering department and take an appropriate interest. Then, suggestions about the operation will not be received defensively, but in a spirit of collaborative care. Encouraging a similar constructive dialogue and interest by your colleagues and your pupils (perhaps by way of the school council) will also contribute to the morale and responsiveness of the catering team. And as a baseline, regular appreciation of their efforts by those taking school meals is not only good manners, but a useful support to you in giving recognition to their vital, daily, contribution to the school's operation.

Whilst the catering team may be some of the more visible support staff, the maintenance and caretaking staff are often amongst the more invisible. Classrooms get cleaned, broken chairs get mended, the heating comes on at the right time, and the site is secure at night all because of their attentiveness. So, take a few minutes at staff meetings and in assemblies to highlight what work has been done in school holidays or after pupils have gone home to make sure you're not the only one paying compliments. Very few schools will be able to employ a large team of specialists, so much of your and the business manager's/bursar's job will be to develop a culture of multi-skilling. But skilled they must be. Almost all areas of maintenance are rightly subject to health and safety legislation and you should make sure that whoever is the immediate line manager of support staff is fully conversant with requirements for working conditions and that everyone involved with maintenance/caretaking is properly trained for what they are asked to do. Otherwise, if an accident happens, you could have an expensive claim on your hands.

Partly because of the work they do and the times at which they do it, the maintenance team are shrewd observers of school life. Whilst they may not always be as understanding as you are about some of the inevitable breakages in classrooms which add to their workload, their intuition about what is going on is worth listening to. Sometimes they will be the most fearless whistle-blowers and see things 'on the ground' which have been hidden from you. If you are loyal to them, they will be fiercely loyal to you and the school.

I have emphasised in this chapter your role in getting everyone to give due recognition to the work of support staff. Most of the time, and no doubt in the vast majority of schools, they are, as noted at the start of this chapter, truly the unsung heroes who will 'go the extra mile' like the best of your teaching staff. All that said, you'll want to make sure that each support department is as efficient as it can be. There can be a tendency for support departments to assert an accretion of 'jobs to be done' – and therefore a perceived need for additional personnel – which cannot go unchecked. Teachers are quick to spot and criticise empire building by support staff with a resultant unhealthy 'them and us' divide. (And sometimes it's the bursar/business manager themselves who is guilty of empire building!). You need to be alert to such feelings. Perhaps some 'jobs to be done', once seen as essential, are now less important and need to be shed from job descriptions. Regular performance management discussions (just as important for support staff as for teaching staff) should include an audit of responsibilities with a close eye on where efficiencies might be found, such as in an upgrade of technology or simply perhaps a rearrangement of working spaces. Above all, then, you need to develop a school culture in which it's clear that slacking on responsibilities lets everyone down. So the more transparent you can be about what everyone does – teaching and support staff – the more you'll have team players rather than empire builders. The analogy of a principal or head being like the conductor of an orchestra is a familiar one. But it's worth keeping it in mind here as you contemplate how your leadership – what you say and what you do, how you set the tone – can best bring together different roles, different skills, some more prominent, some less so, according to different times and different needs in the school year. Skilful attention to the precise contribution of everyone in your 'orchestra' is one of the best ways to promote harmony across the whole organisation.

******

Septimus Hodge has been in post as principal of Sidley Park School (a mixed independent/private school of 1,000 students) for just over a year. He has worked very effectively with the school business manager to control costs and inefficiencies, but is concerned that the head of IT Services appears rarely available to support teaching staff and is often away from school sourcing material for ambitious infrastructure projects, leaving an overstretched IT team.

Septimus plans to address the problem by:

- *Asking the business manager to remind the head of IT services of the need to be part of the team supporting teachers' day-to-day IT needs, with a formal warning to the head of IT services to do so if necessary.*
- *Asking for a dedicated email helpline to be set up to log date/time of support requests and date/time of resolution.*
- *Closer scrutiny of the rationale for IT infrastructure plans in the development plan.*

He encounters the following difficulties:

- *The business manager says the problem is that teachers' requests have become unmanageable for the head of IT services and her team, and that the solution is to take on an additional IT officer to deal with teachers' needs.*
- *The head of IT services refuses to set up an email helpline, maintaining that teachers won't use it. She is also adamant that her frequent attendance at IT conferences and technology fairs is vital to keep the school IT systems up-to-date. The business manager is reluctant to contemplate any disciplinary action against the head of IT services because of her crucial understanding of the school's IT systems.*

To resolve these, he decides to:
- *Agree with the business manager to investigate the need for an additional IT officer if the need can be*

proven, but only when the business manager has taken action to ensure a helpline is set up, scrutinised and curtailed the head of IT services's absences from school, and agreed to take disciplinary action if necessary.
- *Take informal advice about IT development plans from a member of the school board who runs an IT software company.*

Chapter 8
The Wider Community

Neighbours. Other schools. Planners. Local authority. Local newspapers. Alumni. The inspectorate. The national scene.

So far, I have focussed on the people and processes lying most directly within your remit as head or principal. But it's important to remember that you are not only a leader and a figurehead within your school community, but will also have a profile in the wider local community. And you'll not only be called upon to represent your school at a local level, but also to interact with national agencies and organisations.

The reputation of your school in your neighbourhood is vital. Its fortunes can rise and fall on local 'word of mouth'. Immediate neighbours, if they are not parents of current pupils, tend to have mixed views about schools. Some love the sound of children playing; others are annoyed by thoughtless parent parking; some are grateful for the school as a community resource; others are incensed by intrusive building projects. Whilst you could argue that they have chosen to live by a school and should put up with the pros and cons, this is no way to promote neighbourliness. So you'll want to think of ways engaging with them and responding to their concerns. You might start by letting them use the school hall for neighbourhood meetings or sending a special invitation to see the school on an open morning. Such gestures will go a long way to ironing out the niggles about noise or parking. And certainly if you're planning a building project, anticipation of possible objections and early consultation are essential.

If your school adjoins another institution such as a school/college, a care home/hospital, a place of worship, try to find out what their institutional needs are. Are there ways in which you can collaborate? Share some resources? Operate more compatibly? As with so much of leadership, building up mutual support and trust at an early stage will help you to navigate any choppy waters that crop up later. And remember that you'll be served back what you serve up. Don't be surprised if you make a fuss about an aspect of their operation impinging upon yours, then they'll find something to complain about in return.

Even if you don't have another school as a near neighbour, it's wise to get to know other schools in the general locality, as noted in the first chapter. You'll know that there are all sorts of opportunities for joint enterprise, ranging from sports fixtures to professional development sessions and, at a school leader to school leader level, opportunities to compare notes and share concerns. In some circumstances, you may see other schools as competitors and you'll want to keep a wary eye on their policies and developments, with a view to protecting your own USP, whilst of course maintaining a professional cordiality. A good number of schools are grouped together as part of a multi-academy trust, as part of a consortium, or under the general oversight of the local authority or independent/private schools' associations. And why not use your own contacts with leaders/schools you have worked with/in before? If their set-up is similar to yours, but in another part of the country, it's especially helpful to be able to use these contacts to widen your own educational vision and as a source of new ideas.

Co-operation between schools in different sectors has probably never been greater, driven in part by political pressure upon independent schools, especially in the UK, to justify their charitable status. If you're running an independent/private school, you'll want to make sure that your school partnerships are strong and as mutually beneficial as possible: tokenism is not going to cut it. Allowing use of your sports facilities, for example, is just a starter and is one-sided. Are you running joint clubs such as chess or debating? A schools' orchestra? Are there opportunities to combine teaching in subjects such as Latin or a modern language? How about shared tutorials for university/college entrance? Can your colleagues learn about new approaches to teaching and learning from their counterparts in the public/state sector?

Aside from your school connections in the locality, you'll need to form good relationships with key officers in your local authority, not only in the education services. Or at least make sure that colleagues with delegated responsibilities have done so. Establishing good lines of communication with the local safeguarding officer is vital, as is a grasp of how local child medical and welfare services operate. Getting to know the planners and the highway authorities can all prove useful, too, in the multi-faceted nature of your job. If you're running a faith school, what links, besides those formally laid down, do you need to develop with the parent foundation and related faith institutions?

An aspect of local life you probably underestimate is the influence of free newspapers and magazines. Whilst we may imagine that most of them are thrown out straightaway, they do get to every local household in a way that very few advertising campaigns could. And local journalists are hungry for copy. So you, or someone else senior in your team, should get to know the education reporter and give them snappy and well-drafted press releases. A good quality accompanying photo will also be appreciated. Why not offer to write a regular op-ed piece? Good for your and your school's profile in the community and especially nice for current parents to point proudly to 'their school' in print.

Another influential group of people you'll want to get to know are loyal alumni. Not all pupils remember their school days fondly or play an active part in alumni associations, but those who do will be particularly interested in your appointment. Some will worry that major changes will be afoot; others will just be keen to see the school developing and thriving. One of your challenges is to make sure that former students are encouraged to be active supporters of your plans, rather than a self-serving club which does not reflect the current school's priorities. If your school doesn't already have an alumni office, you may want to think about assigning one of your admin staff, or perhaps a recently retired member of the teaching staff (preferably one much-loved by former students), with a brief to enlarge your database of alumni and organise some social events in school which will appeal to a good cross-section of ages and interests. The aim is to tempt more people to visit their old school and meet you and some of your colleagues. On the whole, alumni re-visiting their school (even relatively recent leavers or the inherently cynical) are impressed by how much approaches to teaching and learning and pastoral care have improved. You can then build on this by getting their support as advocates for the school in their circles of friends and colleagues; and, with luck, their financial support too for further development projects.

Mention of inspection or school quality review tends to strike fear into the hearts of teachers. It needn't and indeed shouldn't. A routine visit by school inspectors/reviewers should be seen as a chance to show off the best of the school in action. A chance, as one primary school inspector put it, for 'Show and Tell', not 'Hide and Seek'. An inspection is one of those occasions when your positive leadership will make all the difference. One of your jobs in leading the school is to be the one scanning the horizon, looking ahead beyond the day-to-day. So, as part of maintaining high standards, you will have made meeting statutory requirements and enshrining best practice a top priority. Then an inspection should hold no fears. But, of course, inspections are forensic and the detail of paperwork and policies is all-important. It's the paperwork which teachers often find most irksome about inspection regimes. And it's the paperwork which sometimes lets a school down. So you, the bursar or business manager, and the admin team have an especial responsibility to flag up to teaching staff exactly what is required of them, making systems for record-keeping as simple and painless as possible. You'll need to keep regular checks on how well it's all being done, even if you think you've initiated something pretty fool-proof.

Another way in which your leadership can help in meeting inspections with equanimity is to try as much as possible to understand the process and rationale of inspection and pass those insights on to your staff. In the UK, both OFSTED and ISI publish very clear criteria by which schools are to be judged, as do most review/inspection bodies around the world. Without dominating all that you do, they must inform the framework within which your school operates. If you can digest these and regularly help your staff to find ways of applying them as a matter of course, inspections should run smoothly. It's also your job to make sure that any updates are promulgated in a timely way to staff. Larger schools may have a compliance officer who'll keep everyone posted, but even then, you and your senior team will need to give crucial practical guidance on implementation in your particular setting. Don't forget that the school board will need to be brought in on the process too. Inspectors will need to know that trustees understand their statutory duties, particularly in relation to safeguarding. Again, regular reminders and updates to the board will avoid last-minute panics.

Inspection regulations hardly make enthralling bedtime reading so sometimes it's very helpful to get some more flesh on the bones by booking yourself on to a training course about inspections. Many such courses are readily available. They'll take you through the basic requirements, but just as valuable is the hinterland discussion with fellow school leaders. For a modest outlay, there are a number of companies who will come into school to undertake an audit of your inspection/review readiness: time and money well-spent as another excellent way of gaining a first-hand understanding of it all.

All this takes you outside the immediate bubble of school life. That's a good thing. It's all too easy as a head or principal to focus too intently upon the minutiae of day-to-day school life and not take inspiration from the world outside; or to think that you haven't time to be out of school, or are not setting a good example to your classroom colleagues by taking time to engage with the wider educational scene. You should make time for catching up with latest professional developments. You should make time to write for educational magazines or blogs. You should not be shy of signing up to do keynote addresses at conferences. Make contact with university education departments and find out what they are researching and how it may be of interest to you. In the UK, for instance, the *National Foundation for Education Research* website provides a wealth of information. There may be opportunities for you and your school to get involved in research projects. Keep your knowledge of teaching and learning current by regular reading of a reputable educational journal, or following blogs and listening to podcasts of educationists you respect.

Not only will these be quite simply personally and professionally refreshing, but they will also be great catalysts in crystallising your strategic thinking. That's the subject of the next chapter.

******

Deloris Van Cartier is principal of St Katherine's Elementary School. A former student of the school, who is now a singer with a highly successful band, has given several millions to build a music/performing arts building. Space is limited on the school site, so the architects have designed a narrow four-floor building to make sure play space is not compromised, in accordance with the donor's wishes. Deloris faces objections to the plans from neighbours who say that it will overlook their gardens and be a source of intrusive noise. They have started a well-organised campaign in the local newspaper.

Deloris decides to:

- *Ask the architects to modify the design so that there are no windows overlooking neighbours' gardens.*
- *Consult the donor about losing some play space so the height of the building can be reduced.*
- *Invite the neighbours to come into school to look at the modified plans, to hear a demonstration of proposed soundproofing, and to submit written views via a comment box.*
- *Make plans to open up the building for local use out of school hours.*
- *Talk to the local press about the need for local children to have opportunities to develop musical abilities.*

In carrying out these plans, Deloris finds that:

- *Some windows will have to remain overlooking gardens if every room is to have natural light.*
- *The donor is persuaded that more play space needs to be impinged and contributes a substantial donation towards improved play equipment.*

- *The objections from neighbours have been stirred up by one neighbour in particular.*
- *The local authority is concerned that access out of hours to the new building will be through the school grounds.*

Deloris brings plans to a successful conclusion by:

- *Winning over most of the neighbours by the revised designs, which include a reduced building height, good soundproofing and opaque glass in windows overlooking gardens.*
- *Detailed personal discussion with the neighbour who most objects in order to mitigate their concerns.*
- *Satisfying the local authority's concerns by revised entry routes to the building.*
- *Gaining endorsement in the local press from local community leaders and councillors for the music provision for the wider community.*

Chapter 9
Strategic Planning

Priorities. Positioning yourself in the market. Challenge of local schools – unfair competition. Sharing information. Budgeting. Fundraising. Bursaries/fees. Emergency planning. Future-gazing.

Whilst the first few months of your new job will clearly be about getting to know the detail of what makes the school tick (or not!) and making appropriate immediate changes, one of the most important jobs of a school head or principal, like any leader, is to be out in front scanning the horizon. You'll want to identify priorities for your strategic planning pretty early on. It's one of the huge privileges of the job. You get to make big decisions about how the school is going to shape up in future years: it's an exciting prospect to be approached with imagination and energy.

In some schools, priorities will be forced upon you either by previous neglect or by external factors which suddenly impinge. It's a fact that all schools, whether public or private, maintained or independent, will find themselves in some sort of competitive situation. Public judgement in the form of inspections, reviews, and local word of mouth impact directly on student recruitment with consequent financial implications.

Your strategic planning should start with an honest analysis of where you are in the local (or, in the case of boarding schools, the national and international) pecking order. What is attractive to pupils and parents about your school and what puts them off? As mentioned in the first chapter, you might want to put together an anonymous survey of current and prospective families, or commission a 'mystery shopper' from an external agency. And certainly an 'awayday' with the SLT and the school board early on will help. You'll probably be surprised at the things that are thrown up. Whilst the quality of learning and teaching and pastoral care will be uppermost, practicalities which impact on families' lives such as timings of the school day, after-school provision, flexi-boarding, accessibility by car and/or public transport will no doubt feature and should inform future planning.

And then what distinguishes your school from other similar schools? That USP again. How are you going to maintain a strong reputation? You'll need to have a clear, ongoing, strategy for getting your message out into the community. You'll need to make an early judgement about the most cost-effective way of doing this and who has responsibility for it. Larger independent/private schools may have quite substantial marketing teams and budgets, but you'll want to know if sophisticated and expensive marketing really does the job. In smaller schools, simply making the most of open days where the quality and warmth of interactions between pupils, teaching and support staff is palpable, can be just as effective.

Good leaders always have to make sure they are bringing their followers with them. In your strategic planning, it's crucial to remember this. A plan which has little input from others in your organisation will simply look like your personal 'wish-list' and not have much *strategy* to it. As noted in earlier chapters, schools are not generally places where change is easily embraced, so you'll need to be clear with your various constituencies – pupils, staff, parents and trustees – about the reasoning behind what you are proposing. And then, get perspectives and input about practicalities from those who will be key to implementing the plan. Above all, don't be tempted by short-term fixes to more systemic problems, and keep firm control of how and when you share information more widely. Rumours leaking out about what you're planning will inevitably be misinformed on detail, which could result in negative press before you've prepared the ground properly.

Most plans cost money. So, obviously, your strategic plans need proper budgeting. Here, the business manager/bursar will be of great help and so it's important to get them onside early on and understand your thinking. They will help you to work out how capital costs can be spread over a number of years and will test the priorities of your plan, as well as making suggestions about where savings could be made. But, beware of cutting back on the essentials of teaching and learning to finance a grand plan: servicing the day-to-day needs of the classroom must remain top of your list. That said, as an incoming principal or head, you should take the opportunity to go through the budgeting processes with the business manager/bursar to assure yourself that individual budget-holders are using their allocations efficiently. Some teachers are very good at managing budgets; others are not and may need the finance department's especial help and scrutiny. This in turn will help them buy-in (literally) to strategic budgetary planning instead of more opportunistic expenditure.

Most schools have fundraising schemes to supplement their usual streams of income. In large independent/private schools, fundraising can run into millions for a bursary scheme or a new building. In small schools or maintained/state schools, the fundraising is most unlikely to run into millions, but will be no less important in funding things which cannot otherwise be afforded through your capitation budget. And clearly the scale of your fundraising operation will be reflected in how many personnel are assigned to it. Large schools may have a dedicated fundraising department; in smaller schools, you may well find that you have to take a lead in this with help from your support staff. You'll also find that teachers are willing to do their bit for fundraising, if they believe it will directly help their students. But however large or small your school, you should work out the best strategies for fundraising. Is it confined to parents alone or can you get support from local businesses? And can you easily get in touch with alumni who would help you?

Whilst on the subject of finance, it's worth drawing attention to some strategies for setting fees if you're heading up a fee-paying school. Rightly, this is a shared duty with the bursar/business manager and the school board. But your job is to make sure that fee-setting isn't just a budgetary exercise, but also reflects the aims and mission of the school. The board will have an awareness of local/national competition and demographics, but you'll want to influence strategic decisions about the balance between top-of-the-range resources and affordability. Such decisions very much determine the sort of school, the sort of students, and the sort of parents you're likely to attract, with a consequent effect upon the profile and values of the school's operation.

Intimately linked with fees is the provision of bursaries and projects demonstrating community benefit. Virtually all independent/private schools wish and need to demonstrate their social commitment in this way. But be careful to think through your plans for funding this. Whilst a majority of parents are inherently supportive of such outreach (and will understand the political imperatives), many will be stretched already in paying fees and won't want to feel that there is extensive outflow of resources which do not directly benefit their child. So, creative long-term planning to identify other sources of income will be vital. And as with so many areas of school life, you'll probably be the one to kick-start the ideas.

Perhaps one of the most galling things for a principal/head to have to deal with in strategic planning is the response to external factors which at first seem beyond your control. For instance, you might find that a neighbouring school changes its intake policy in a way which potentially affects your recruitment; or what once seemed your school's USP is now imitated by others. Or what if public transport to your school's neighbourhood is suddenly reduced or axed? Whilst a certain initial sense of irritation and despondency are natural reactions to such challenges, this is when your creativity and forward-thinking leadership skills are most needed. Don't be defensive. It's an opportunity to reinvent or reinvigorate your school's USP or, for example, embrace a plan for greener transport solutions. Sometimes, these external factors are a catalyst for changes which might have been at the back of your mind, but previously seemed too radical. Now is the time to be bold!

You need to be constantly thinking about what the future may look like, not only in one year's time but in the next five to ten years. It's easy to fall into the trap of thinking that a five-year development plan, focussing chiefly on human and material resources, does that job. But you need to be much more adventurous and wide-ranging in your thinking. You'll know all too well that the landscape can change very fast either locally or even nationally. However well organised you are, however many good policies you have in place, events can overtake you. Things that you might have mentally assessed as low risk, turn out to have a high impact. School leaders who look creatively ahead are much better prepared for changes which suddenly come into sharp focus. In the Covid pandemic, to take an example which suddenly impacted on all schools, places which had already begun to embrace some remote/online teaching and resources were in a much stronger position. Taking time to work out how latest educational ideas might be applied in your school is time well-spent if you're really to be ahead of the curve. Don't be afraid to pinch good ideas from elsewhere (respecting intellectual property rights of course), but equally have the courage not to go with the latest fad if it doesn't fit well with your school's ethos. But perhaps keep it in the back of your mind in case circumstances change. A fundamental question to ask yourself at the start of your new job is how you see learning and teaching developing over the following decade. What does that mean for the way in which your school is organised? Will you need to begin to make evolutionary changes? Work out the direction of travel to have some insight into the destination.

One obvious area to consider is how the ever-growing capability and application of technology will not only impact on how pupils learn, but on what they learn, and how they exercise good judgement as we prepare them for the world in which they will work and use their leisure time. There was a time when smart phones didn't exist. There was a time when very few people owned a computer. Today, a significant proportion of the world's population has a handheld computer in the form of a phone which has well over 100,000 times the processing power of the computer that landed humans on the moon. I am sure that most school leaders of that era would have ridiculed the idea of computers of such power being commonplace in student's pockets. With a constant need to demonstrate careful housekeeping, schools are inherently cautious institutions, but this example demonstrates the need to think big, to think 'what if'? And then think what should we be doing now to harness such exciting potential for good in the future, rather than feeling defensive and hoping it will go away? It won't!

Perhaps linked with the proliferation of social media which smart phones have facilitated, there are increasingly rapid changes in social and cultural norms and expectations. If you're to do your best by your students, you'll want to spend some of your future-gazing time thinking about what this might mean for developing the curriculum, the values you and your teachers are projecting, and the overall life of the school community. You'll need to be alert to how you help students (and indeed their parents) respond to the complexities of the society in which they are growing up.

Much better to have some plans – however sketchily formed to begin with – than have to resort to complete knee-jerk reactions as events overtake you.

That said, there will always be times and events in school life which call for plans to be drawn up rapidly in response. Strategy doesn't go out of the window at that point: far from it. The decisions you make in times of emergency can have a profound long-term effect. So you'll need to draw up clear policies for the obvious emergencies such as the sudden death of a pupil or a member of staff. But you'll also need to plan by imagining a scenario where you have to spend every waking hour with your senior team working out solutions to something completely unforeseen. The practicalities of this need to be considered so that the ongoing running of the school is not neglected and you are not a sleep-deprived zombie. When you think of the demands that the Covid pandemic made, you'll know this is not a fanciful exaggeration. In sum, then, your key strategy is to plan to navigate and embrace high challenge and enable others to do the same. Any such challenges then become low threat and you will have shown that you have scanned the horizon for your team as effectively as you can.

******

Hugh Evans has just become head of Windsor High School (a non-selective private day school for girls aged 4-11 with 250 students). Numbers in the school are falling and recruitment is not encouraging. The school board is concerned and has made it clear that Hugh must draw up immediate measures to address the problem.

Hugh decides to:

- *Ask his PA to tabulate exit data to learn more about students who are leaving before Year 6 (the final year group) and the schools to which they are going.*
- *Conduct an anonymous survey of parents to get an assessment of the school's strengths and weaknesses.*
- *Employ a 'mystery shopper' to compare the experience of recruitment at his school with other local schools.*
- *Hold a school board/SLT awayday to discuss his findings and understand more about the potential attractions of rival schools.*

As a result, Hugh discovers that:

- *The majority of students leaving are going to a mixed junior school which feeds into a highly academic senior school, with a few going to the (free) local primary school.*
- *In the survey, a number of parents mentioned that teachers do not regularly set homework at the times prescribed, and are unresponsive to email.*
- *Enquiries for places are not dealt with systematically. The 'mystery shopper' had to wait over a week for a response to her phone message and email enquiry.*
- *SLT colleagues feel that rewards and sanctions are not consistently applied in the younger years.*

In the light of this, Hugh adopts the following plans:

- *Review and amend policies on homework and rewards and sanctions and give due notice to staff that these need to be consistently applied. He asks the SLT to keep a particular eye on these areas.*
- *Ensure the policy on email response to parents is workable and remind staff that swift responses (even holding responses) build up good relationships; slow responses leave matters to fester.*
- *Ask his PA to investigate the process for dealing with enquiries for places to find out where the delays lie.*
- *Sound out the business manager about the possibility of further administrative assistance for admissions, making the case for the need 'to speculate to accumulate'.*
- *Identify the weaknesses in rival schools' offerings (e.g. over-emphasis on academic success at the expense of wellbeing; or large class sizes) and advertise his school's contrasting strengths (e.g. wide range of extra-curricular activities and attentive pastoral care in small classes).*

Chapter 10
Looking After Yourself

Pace yourself. Links with family and friends. Professional links. Professional associations. Getting out and about. Getting perspective. Personal wellbeing. Nice letters. Don't take it personally. Head's treats.

The fact that principals or heads typically have hundreds of interactions during a school day with people who will want something of you, or want to ask you to help them solve a problem, is undoubtedly emotionally demanding. It can be a lonely role when the buck stops with you; and there can be a sense of feeling constantly judged. But that is the nature of leadership. Nonetheless, it's important to recognise that you need to take specific steps to manage the demands of the job if you are to remain an effective leader. You need to take responsibility for your own wellbeing and, in doing so, you are not shirking your commitment to the school: quite the reverse.

First of all, it goes without saying, then, that the job of a school leader is both exhilarating and potentially exhausting. In term-time, no two days are the same and each can bring new challenges and perspectives which demand your rapid attention. And as your colleagues keenly anticipate a break after the end of a long term, you will still have policy documents to read, budgets to scrutinise, phone calls and emails to attend to, as well as ensuring that all is in order for the coming term/academic year. There's always something to think about. So, switching off and pacing yourself are vital. Take an early check on the pattern of your working day in term-time. If you're a morning person, you may wish to get in before most of your colleagues and get an uninterrupted start on the admin of the day. But you can't burn the candle at both ends and do admin in the evening as well, unless there is something of an emergency. If you're running a boarding school, you'll need to put in an appearance in the evening, so make sure you look at the overall balance of the day and build in time at least to take a walk away from the office. And maybe get one of your deputies to do the early start if you're more of a night owl. You need to be strict with yourself and, if necessary, enlist the help of your PA to enforce your regime. If you're living on or near the school site, don't be tempted to pop into the office to check something unless it really can't wait until the next day.

The same goes for the overall pattern of the school year. There are bound to be pressure points when your diary is likely to be exceptionally full, such as report-writing near the end of term. Flag these up with your PA and other colleagues well ahead, so that expectations about the calls on your time are appropriately managed. Equally, don't forget to plan the working pattern of the school holidays. It's healthy to take a break from emails and phone calls and again, with the trusty support of your PA, you'll soon know what is practical and possible according to your own circumstances. It's all very well to exhort pupils to take time to recharge the batteries over the summer and endorse relaxed summer reading, but are you doing the same in preparation for the new academic year?

Second, given that the job can be a lonely one, all school leaders need a few soul-mates. Here, family and friends are vital supporters: most immediately, you'll need people with whom you can have a regular, honest, conversation and offload the joys and sorrows of the day. That's often going to be a spouse or partner, or trusted family member or friend, who'll no doubt become a sympathetic and understanding ear, even if occasionally their empathy for school life wears a little thin! But, as a telephone advertising slogan once put it, 'it's good to talk'. More widely, a circle of friends disconnected from school life can also be supportive in a very different way, taking you away from your immediate concerns and engaging you with different outlooks. But this needs to be worked at: it's sometimes quite disconcerting that a whole school term can slip by without much wider social contact because you've been too tired or preoccupied to initiate it.

It's a good idea to belong to a professional association: one which is specifically for school leaders. Not only will their publications and conferences give you some useful professional development as well as legal advice and protection in the case of difficulties, but they are a way of meeting others who are doing a similar job and sharing experiences. Whilst you might imagine such interactions will be informed by lofty educational discussion, it's often the chat about the minutiae of school business which predominates.

The sense of solidarity in this is wonderfully consoling and an antidote to the loneliness of leadership.

Not only is it good for your wellbeing to talk with others, but it's very restorative to make time, however briefly, for a sociable interest outside school. You might want to play some team sport, take up a fitness class, or join a running club, a choir or an orchestra. All health-giving in different ways. On the other hand, you might want to immerse yourself in something which doesn't require interaction with people (you have that all the time in school), so making time for a long walk, or enjoying a good book or film, or listening to music, might be your preferred diversion. But the important point is to make sure that you take deliberate steps to do these things and that you don't feel guilty about doing so.

In sum then, much of looking after yourself as a school leader is making sure you are able to stand back from the daily busyness and get a perspective on the job. As has been noted, in so many ways being a principal or head requires constant reaction to events and so, from the outset, you'll need a mindset to embrace this. Each day could well bring a new problem to solve, a new idea to digest. Part of the satisfaction of the job is using your experience and wisdom to get the best possible outcomes to these for all involved. But, if you're to retain a sense of perspective, you'll need to recognise that not all outcomes will be entirely as you would wish. Don't waste time and mental energy seeking for perfection when pragmatism is the best answer.

Another way of keeping everything in perspective is to make sure, as far as possible, that your diary has a deliberate balance of different types of interactions each school day. And be conscious of enjoying the privileges of leadership: the strategic macro-thinking; being able to see students of all ages in action in and outside the classroom; being able to give praise to colleagues for work well done. Given that you are responsible to all the different constituencies mentioned in this book, as well as to yourself and to your family and friends, it's imperative to try to give them all some attention each day. Some will predominate on some days more than others, but the principle is a good one.

One of the aspects of headship which is perhaps surprising to many is that you are personally identified with every aspect of school life. To paraphrase the French king, Louis XIV, it feels as if 'l'ecole c'est moi' (I myself am the school). Now I'm sure very few school leaders see the job as an ego-trip – indeed things will almost certainly go wrong if you do. So sometimes that personal identification with all that goes on is hard to bear. Whilst you must take responsibility for all that happens on your watch, it's not healthy to take everything as personal criticism or praise. You'll know when you deserve personal praise or criticism and deal with it appropriately. But equally, just as you wouldn't take credit for others' successes, you shouldn't always blame yourself for others' shortcomings, but do your best to help them out as any good leader should.

Finally, take time to enjoy what one school leader has called 'head's treats'. Treats, by definition, should be limited (that's what makes them fun): the absentee leader who always seems to be away on self-indulgent outings quickly earns the scorn of the rest of the staff. But by virtue of your office, you're likely to be invited to local civic events or lunch with another local head or principal, or maybe a residential conference which allows for more extended reflection than a rushed INSET day course. And of course, you have the flexibility in your day-to-day diary to be able to accept such invitations. Whilst these are all opportunities for developing professional contacts, they are also times away from the hurly-burly of school which you should not feel guilty about enjoying. Make the occasional lunch a leisurely one; put your deputy firmly in charge while you're away and resist the temptation to look at emails. You will then return to school refreshed by even this smallest change of scene and pace.

******

Minerva McGonagall has been principal of Potter Academy for just over a term. She has spent many years in senior leadership, but this is her first appointment as principal. An inspection/school review under the previous principal identified a number of shortcomings which Minerva has worked ceaselessly to address. The school board is delighted with her work, but the chair has expressed his concern that she has had little time for anything aside from immediate school matters, and has urged her to make time for her own recreation.

Minerva decides to:

- *Ask her PA to block out the equivalent of a lesson a day to allow for wider educational reading. Matters arising, unless urgent, are to be dealt with by her deputy.*
- *Make sure she walks around the school at break time, talking to pupils once a day.*

- *Asking a fellow principal in her locality to be a mentor with whom she can 'let off steam'.*
- *Join the local dance class.*
- *Make a concerted effort to plan treats during school holidays with family and friends well in advance, making sure that her PA handles emails during her absence, sending holding replies if necessary.*

The following considerations arise:

- *The protected time in her diary for educational reading is frequently interrupted by 'urgent' matters.*
- *Teachers will often use a break time encounter to monopolise her attention.*
- *The local dance class is full of current school parents.*

She resolves these by:

- *Making it clear to her PA and her deputy that there can be very few matters which require her immediate response and she will keep her office door firmly closed during her protected reading time.*
- *Explaining to teachers that her break time walks are to meet pupils but that they are welcome to talk informally with her over lunch or drop into her office if her door is open.*
- *Joining a dance class in a different neighbourhood.*

Conclusion

This book has aimed to guide you through some of the 'nuts and bolts' of the job and some of the scenarios you will encounter. Some of it may sound daunting, but once you're doing the job, you'll find that a combination of your wisdom, instinct, and experience mean that you'll get it right most of the time. You'll aim to keep the school in even better shape than you found it as you respond to all that crops up. And, as you see the tangible benefits of that for everyone in the school community, you'll find it's immensely rewarding and satisfying. Your ability to see ahead, to solve problems, to say and do the right thing at the right time, will make a positive difference to many people's lives.

As a teacher you are a 'people person' and being a head or principal takes this onto another level. It's a huge privilege to be responsible not only for pupils in an individual classroom, but for the overall wellbeing of the school. It's a big job, and a challenging one, which will make intellectual, physical and emotional demands upon you in ways you'd perhaps never have imagined. The qualities required of a successful school leader are myriad: whatever else, you'll certainly need resilience and huge energy. And in times of uncertainty or crisis, your whole community will look to you for certainty and direction. But as with facing any challenge, you'll have a goal in sight, an aim and a plan which will help to carry you through the tougher bits.

However much you've read up on the job and, I hope, taken on board some the insights of this book, you need to be psychologically prepared to expect the unexpected. Most human beings are short-termist in their thinking and we're not usually prepared to invest time, mental energy or money in something which may be a remote possibility. School leaders tend to be eternal optimists (we believe in the promise of the next generation), thinking that even though, over time, the chances of a disaster are quite large (a pandemic of the Covid sort was really likely one day) it won't happen soon and it won't happen to us. So there's a crucial balance to be obtained between gloomily expecting and planning for a whole raft of remote possibilities, and travelling more optimistically, but expecting and believing you will have the energy and capacity to respond skilfully to something for which you have not planned. If you over-worry about future doom, you may miss the fulfilment of the present.

Fundamentally, you'll know that schools are wonderful places in which to work: there's a real joy in working with children and young people, and with the supportive camaraderie of colleagues, however frustrating they can all be at times. Equally, there's something about the fixed rhythms of school life – the daily timetable, the rituals of the start and end of term, the annual celebratory events – which are uniquely enjoyable. But in running the school, you're privileged to have all that and more. For you now, this will be overlaid by the fact that no two days in term will be quite the same: there will always be new pleasures, interests and challenges as part of a job which calls upon such a variety of skills and personal attributes.

Furthermore, there's no need to feel any guilt at enjoying being a leader, provided you're aware of the dangers of becoming remote or despotic. You can legitimately take pleasure in putting your ideas into action and passing on your values and attributes. You have the considerable power to make a difference and it's right that you should be able to feel that quiet glow of pleasure when you see positive outcomes for ideas and projects you have initiated. That is why you wanted to do the job in the first place and why, if you're prepared to throw yourself wholeheartedly into it, it's one of the most satisfying and rewarding jobs in the world.